THE ESCALATION OF AMERICAN INVOLVEMENT IN THE VIETNAM WAR

THE ESCALATION OF AMERICAN INVOLVEMENT IN THE VIETNAM WAR

MASON CREST

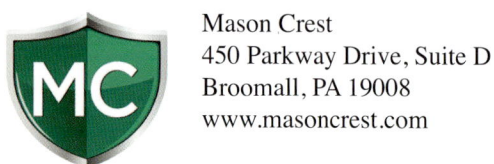

Mason Crest
450 Parkway Drive, Suite D
Broomall, PA 19008
www.masoncrest.com

© 2018 by Mason Crest, an imprint of National Highlights, Inc.

All rights reserved. No part of this publication may be reproduced or transmitted in any form or by any means, electronic or mechanical, including photocopying, recording, taping, or any information storage and retrieval system, without permission in writing from the copyright holder.

Cataloging-in-Publication Data on file with the Library of Congress.

Printed and bound in the United States of America.

First printing
9 8 7 6 5 4 3 2 1

ISBN: 978-1-4222-3889-9
Series ISBN: 978-1-4222-3887-5
ebook ISBN: 978-1-4222-7899-4
ebook series ISBN: 978-1-4222-7897-0

Produced by Regency House Publishing Limited
The Manor House
High Street
Buntingford
Hertfordshire
SG9 9AB
United Kingdom

www.regencyhousepublishing.com

Text copyright © 2018 Regency House Publishing Limited/Christopher Chant.

PAGE 2: Da Nang, Vietnam. A young Marine private waits on the beach during the Marine landing.

PAGE 3: President Lyndon B. Johnson. National Security meeting on Vietnam in the Cabinet Room of the White House.

RIGHT: The radar operator aboard a U.S. Navy Martin SP-5B Marlin from Patrol Squadron 40 (VP-40) helps guide his aircraft towards an unidentified surface contact off the coast of Vietnam as part of Operation Market Time, June 1965.

PAGE 6: Arrival of the U.S. 1st Cavalry Division (Air Mobile) in Vietnam consisting of 15,800 men and 424 helicopters and aircraft.

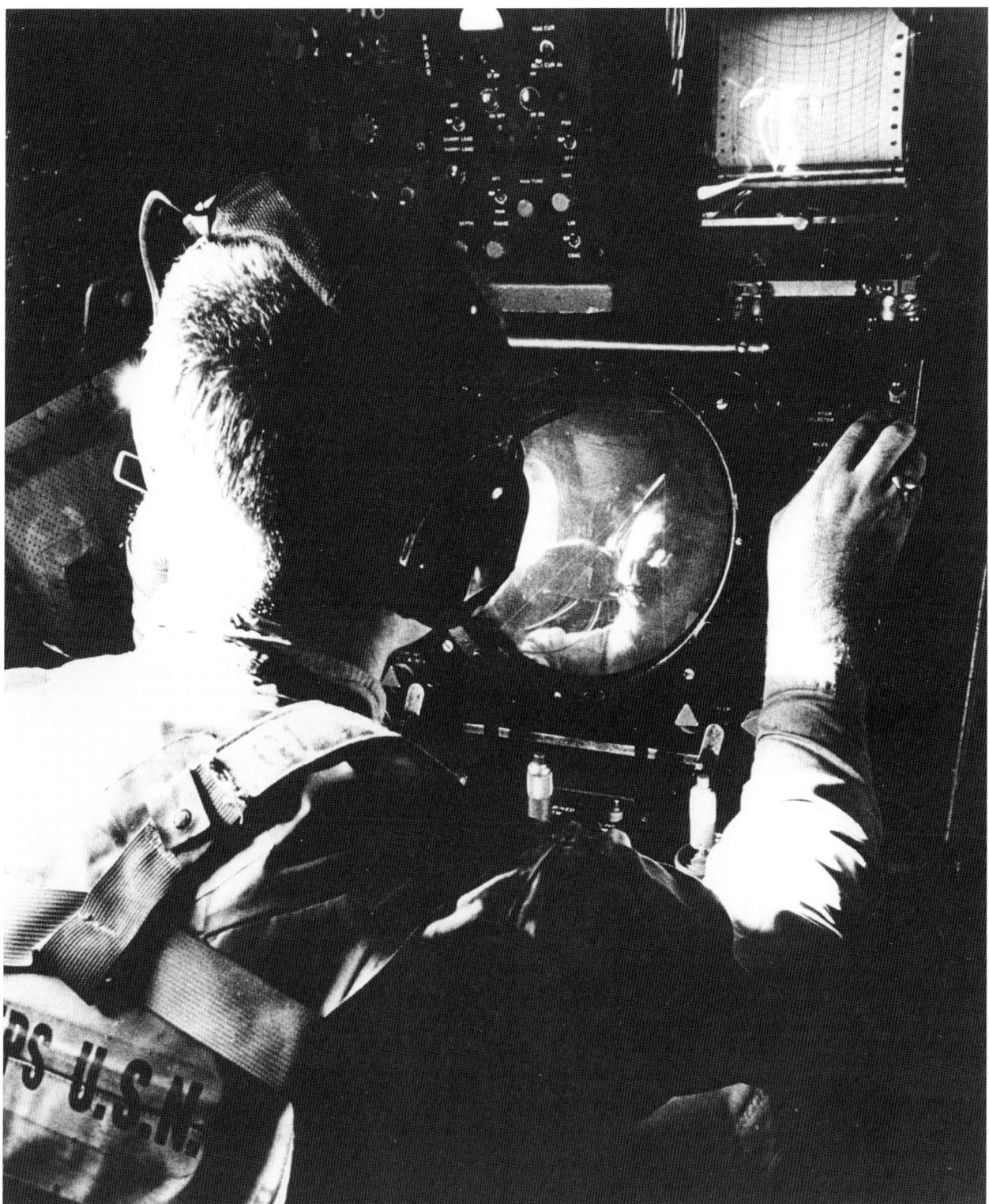

TITLES IN THE VIETNAM WAR SERIES:

The Origins of Conflict in the Vietnam War
The Escalation of American Involvement in the Vietnam War
The U.S. Ground War in Vietnam 1965–1973
Stalemate: U.S. Public Opinion of the War in Vietnam
The Fall of Saigon and the End of the Vietnam War

CONTENTS

Vietnam Veterans Memorial Wall 10

Chapter One:
The Gulf of Tonkin Incident 12

Chapter Two:
"Rolling Thunder" 40

Time Line of the Vietnam War 72

Series Glossary of Key Terms 74

Further Reading and Internet Resources 75

Index 76

Further Information 80

KEY ICONS TO LOOK FOR:

Words to Understand: These words with their easy-to-understand definitions will increase the reader's understanding of the text, while building vocabulary skills.

Sidebars: This boxed material within the main text allows readers to build knowledge, gain insights, explore possibilities, and broaden their perspectives by weaving together additional information to provide realistic and holistic perspectives.

Educational Videos: Readers can view videos by scanning our QR codes, providing them with additional content to supplement the text. Examples include news coverage, moments in history, speeches, iconic sports moments, and much more!

Text-Dependent Questions: These questions send the reader back to the text for more careful attention to the evidence presented here.

Research Projects: Readers are pointed toward areas of further inquiry connected to each chapter. Suggestions are provided for projects that encourage deeper research and analysis.

Series Glossary of Key Terms: This back-of-the-book glossary contains terminology used throughout the series. Words found here increase the reader's ability to read and comprehend high-level books and articles in this field.

OPPOSITE: Guerrillas assembling shells and rockets supplied and delivered via the Ho Chi Minh Trail.

Vietnam Veterans Memorial

The Vietnam Veterans Memorial was designed by Maya Lin, a 21-year-old from Athens, Ohio. It was unveiled with an opening ceremony in 1982 in Washington, D.C.

The memorial is dedicated to the men and women in the U.S. military who served in the war zone of Vietnam. The names of the 58,000 Americans who gave their lives and service to their country are etched chronologically in gabbro stone and listed on the two walls which make up the memorial monument. Those who died in action are denoted by a diamond, those who were missing (MIAs, POWs, and others) are denoted with a cross. When the death of one, who was previously missing is confirmed, a diamond is superimposed over a cross.

The wall consists of two sections, one side points to the Lincoln Memorial and the other to the Washington Monument. There is a pathway along the base for visitors to walk and reflect, or view the names of their loved ones.

When visiting the memorial many take a piece of paper, and using a crayon or soft pencil make a memento of their loved one. This is known as "rubbing." The shiny wall was designed to reflect a visitor's face while reading the names of the military personnel who lost their lives. The idea is that symbolically the past and present are represented. The memorial was paid for by the Vietnam Veterans Memorial Fund, Inc. who raised nearly $9,000,000 to complete it.

The memorial site also includes The Three Servicemen statue built in 1984. The statue depicts three soldiers, purposefully identifiable as *European American, African American,* and *Hispanic American.* The statue faces the wall with the soldiers looking on in solemn tribute at the names of their fallen comrades.

The Vietnam Women's Memorial is dedicated to the women of the United States who served in the Vietnam War, most of whom were nurses. It serves as a reminder of the importance of women in the conflict.

The Vietnam Veterans Memorial can be found to the north of the Lincoln Memorial near the intersection of 22nd St. and Constitution Ave. NW. The memorial is maintained by the U.S. National Park Service, and receives approximately 5 million visitors each year. It is open 24 hours a day and is free to all visitors.

Chapter One
THE GULF OF TONKIN INCIDENT

On July 27, 1964 the Johnson administration ordered the dispatch to South Vietnam of another 5,000 military advisers, so raising the total to 21,000. Shortly after this there occurred the "Gulf of Tonkin incident," which took the form of two "attacks" by North Vietnamese naval forces on a pair of U.S. Navy destroyers, the *Maddox* on August 2 and the *Turner Joy* two days later, steaming in international waters within the Gulf of Tonkin. Later findings, including a National Security Agency report, released in 2005, strongly suggests that the second attack did not in fact take place, as had long been believed, but also attempted to refute the equally long-standing belief that

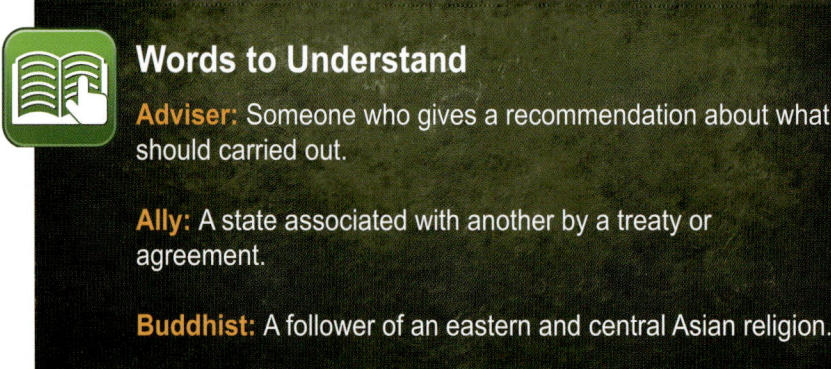

Words to Understand

Adviser: Someone who gives a recommendation about what should carried out.

Ally: A state associated with another by a treaty or agreement.

Buddhist: A follower of an eastern and central Asian religion.

members of the Johnson administration had knowingly lied about the incident. At the time, the Gulf of Tonkin incident persuaded the U.S. Congress to pass the South-East Asia Resolution ("Gulf of Tonkin Resolution") giving the president the authority to assist any country of South-East Asia threatened by "Communist aggression." The resolution also gave President Johnson the legal right to increase the U.S. involvement in the Vietnam conflict, all of which took place less than a year after Johnson had become president. It was the preceding Kennedy administration which had begun to dispatch military advisers to South Vietnam, and Kennedy himself had

LEFT: North Vietnamese P-4 under fire from USS *Maddox* (August 2, 1964).

OPPOSITE ABOVE: A Douglas A-1 aircraft of the USAF on active service in Vietnam, photographed from the cockpit of a U.S. warplane. A North Vietnamese Mikoyan-Guryevich jet-powered fighter breaks away to port.

OPPOSITE BELOW: A member of a USAF Air Commando C-44 unit loads a battery of speakers onto the aircraft in preparation for a psychological warfare mission.

The Escalation of American Involvement in the Vietnam War

.quite quickly begun to reconsider the suitability of this U.S. move, largely as a result of his increasing perception of the Diem administration's corruption and abuse of civil rights, in combination with the South Vietnamese forces' revealed incompetence and steadfast refusal even to consider ways of redressing the situation. Just before his assassination, Kennedy had begun to reduce the number of U.S. advisers, but Johnson believed that it was essential for the USA to challenge what was perceived to be the latest stage in Soviet expansionism, and therefore supported the growth of U.S. involvement in Vietnam to prevent the domino effect from gaining momentum.

As far as the Gulf of Tonkin was concerned, this was the area in which a program of clandestine attacks on North Vietnam had been initiated during 1961 as Operation 34A. The program was initially supervised by

The Gulf of Tonkin Incident

ABOVE: Captain Herrick and Commander Ogier aboard USS *Maddox* (DD-731) in August 1964.

LEFT: USS *Maddox*.

OPPOSITE: Ulysses Simpson Grant Sharp Jr. (April 2, 1906 – December 12, 2001) was a United States Navy four star admiral who served as Commander in Chief, United States Pacific Fleet from 1963–1964; and Commander in Chief, United States Pacific Command from 1964–1968. He was PACOM Commander during the Gulf of Tonkin Incident.

the CIA, but in 1964 was transferred to the Department of Defense, operated by the Studies and Operations Group of what was now the Military Assistance Command, Vietnam. The program involved many elements, but for the naval part the USA had bought from Norway a number of Tjeld-class fast-attack craft and had shipped them to South Vietnam. The craft were manned by South Vietnamese crews, but their operational use was supervised directly by Admiral Ulysses S. Grant Sharp, commander-in-chief of the U.S. Pacific Fleet, his headquarters being in Honolulu, Hawai.

Once the attacks on its coast had begun, North Vietnam protested to the International Control Commission, set up in 1954 to police the terms of the Geneva Accords, but the USA denied any involvement. Four years later, however, the Secretary of Defense, Robert S. McNamara, revealed to the Congress that U.S. Navy destroyers had co-operated with the South Vietnamese FACs in their attacks on the North Vietnamese coast. Although her captain knew of the operations, the *Maddox* was not directly involved.

At the time of the Gulf of Tonkin incident, U.S.-trained South Vietnamese commandos were active in the area: operating from Da Nang, just to the south of the DMZ, in the ex-Norwegian FACs, these commandos made attacks in the Gulf of Tonkin area on the nights of July 31 and August 3. In the first of these undertakings, the commandos attacked a radio transmitter on the island of Hon Nieu, and in the second bombarded a radar site at Cape Vinh Son with a cannon on the FAC. The North Vietnamese responded by attacking warships in the area, of which the most evident was the *Maddox*, which was undertaking an electronic intelligence-gathering mission in the Gulf of Tonkin under the local command of Admiral George Stephen Morrison on the aircraft carrier *Bon Homme Richard*. On August 2 the *Maddox* was attacked by three North Vietnamese P-4-class torpedo boats some 28 miles (45 km) off the North Vietnamese coast in international waters. The *Maddox* evaded a torpedo attack and opened fire with her 127-mm (5 inch) guns, forcing the torpedo craft to withdraw.

15

The Gulf of Tonkin Incident

Warplanes from the carrier USS *Ticonderoga* then attacked the North Vietnamese craft as they pulled back, claiming to have sunk one of them and badly damaging another; in fact none of the craft was sunk. The *Maddox*, which had been hit by only one 14.5-mm (0.57 inch) heavy machine gun round, headed south toward South Vietnamese waters, and was there joined by the *Turner Joy*.

On August 4 another sortie into the waters off North Vietnam was begun by the two destroyers, under the command of Captain John J. Herrick, with orders to approach no closer than 11 miles (18 km) to the North Vietnamese coast. The destroyers detected radar and radio signals suggesting, it was believed, that the North Vietnamese navy was about to make another attack. For some two hours the ships fired on radar targets, maneuvering within the context of electronic and visual reports of hostile craft, but shortly after this Herrick signaled that an attack might not have been attempted, and that there may actually have been no North Vietnamese vessels in the area. There followed an exchange of signals which failed to produce any reliable information, but the crew of the *Maddox* was sure that an attack had

ABOVE: Camp Trai Trung Sup, in South Vietnam, the 3rd Corps Basic Training Center for the Civilian Irregular Defense Group (CIDG), devised by the CIA in early 1961 to counter expanding Viet Cong influence in South Vietnam's Central Highlands, is commanded by the Vietnamese Special Forces (LLDB) and advised by Detachment A, 5th US Special Forces. Here, Sgt. Alvin J. Rouly supervises CIDG trainees firing M-79 grenade-launchers.

The Escalation of American Involvement in the Vietnam War

ABOVE: Members of the 1st Special Forces and Vietnamese volunteers watch grenades exploding during a practice run atop Nui Ba Den in 1964.

LEFT: Photo taken from USS *Maddox* during the Gulf of Tonkin incident, showing three North Vietnamese motor torpedo boats.

The Gulf of Tonkin Incident

taken place, and the "reality" of the attack also began to gain credence in Washington.

Thus warplanes were launched from the aircraft carriers *Ticonderoga* and *Constellation* to attack North Vietnamese torpedo boat bases and fuel facilities. These were ordered by Johnson, who was facing an election that year, and who addressed the nation on television that same day. Although the *Maddox* had been providing passive intelligence support for South Vietnamese attacks at Hon Me and Hon Ngu, McNamara denied to the Congress that the U.S. Navy had actively supported South Vietnamese military operations in the Gulf of Tonkin. McNamara claimed, therefore, that the North Vietnamese attacks were "unprovoked" as the ships had been in international waters. He also claimed that there was irrefutable proof that an unprovoked second attack had been made on the *Maddox*.

On August 7 the Congress passed the joint Gulf of Tonkin Resolution, giving Johnson the authority to conduct military operations in South-East Asia without any declaration of war, and granting him permission "to take all necessary steps, including the use of armed force, to assist any member or protocol state of the Southeast Asia Collective Defense Treaty requesting assistance in defense of its freedom."

The Gulf of Tonkin incident thus marked the beginning of major U.S. military intervention in the Vietnam War. At this stage of the conflict, it should be noted that the number of insurgents in South Vietnam was in the order of 100,000, a huge rise from

RIGHT: Forward air control aircraft (FACS) of the USAF.

The Escalation of American Involvement in the Vietnam War

The Gulf of Tonkin Incident

the commonly accepted figure of 5,000–10,000 in 1959. Conventional military wisdom suggests that the efforts of ten conventional soldiers were required to defeat one insurgent, and the U.S. was therefore committing itself to an effort needing more men that the U.S. Army could ever hope to deploy to South Vietnam.

On the eve of his re-election as president during the first week of November 1964, Johnson established an inter-agency working group to explore all the options available to the U.S. in South Vietnam. Johnson did not wish to enlarge the war, either geographically or in the USA's overall commitment, but did appreciate that another approach was required to

ABOVE: The U.S. deployed planes on leaflet drop missions as the most efficient way of conveying information to the Vietnamese people.

LEFT: Sgt. Thomas G. Gallant, of Detachment A, 5th Special Forces Group, shows a Vietnamese soldier's wife the right way to care for his wounded foot, so that he can avoid making constant trips to the dispensary at Camp Bunard.

OPPOSITE: An American adviser and his South Vietnamese companions keep a sharp lookout for possible guerrilla attack as they cruise along a river near the Cambodian border. The troops were en route to a suspected Viet Cong encampment, where they burned buildings and destroyed cattle and food supplies. The menfolk were missing, but the community's women and children were evacuated from the area.

The Escalation of American Involvement in the Vietnam War

spur the South Vietnamese into greater and more effective action. The two main problems here were, of course, the fact that the South Vietnamese administration was beset by factional strife, and that the South Vietnamese army was achieving little if anything against the Viet Cong. Yet the situation was not so much static as deteriorating rapidly, and the rate of its deterioration would surely increase; it was believed, on the basis of MACV intelligence, that the Communists were moving men and matériel into South Vietnam at an increasing rate. Johnson's feeling that a moment of decision was at hand was mirrored by the U.S. public at large. By mid-November 1964 polls were now showing that the U.S. population had the matter of Vietnam near to the top of the list of problems needing to be resolved. Yet the U.S. seemed to have available to it little in the way of options, which were either to spur the South Vietnamese into effective reform and more capable military action, or itself assume the leadership of military affairs in South Vietnam.

Speculation about South Vietnam was increased when, on November 27, Maxwell D. Taylor, the U.S. ambassador in South Vietnam, arrived in the US for talks. The Department of State claimed that they were merely routine, but U.S. journalists swiftly appreciated that something altogether more important was in the air, and suggested that Taylor would recommend an escalation of the U.S. commitment to the Vietnam War. To many, this seemed to be a course pregnant with the possibility of disaster, for if the course of events to date had provided absolute proof of anything, it was that it was impossible to rely on the South Vietnamese; but even to those who had a sense of impending doom, there appeared to be no realistic alternative to an increased U.S. commitment, as a withdrawal would have crippled the U.S.'s worldwide reputation for reliability and the support of its allies.

21

Taylor did suggest an increased U.S. commitment, if only as a means of improving South Vietnamese morale. But Johnson was firmly of the belief that the U.S. should escalate its presence only if political stability in South Vietnam was improved, and Taylor recommended a compromise solution. The presidential working group had recommended a series of plans incorporating a carefully considered series of graduations in the intensification of a U.S. air campaign against the Communists, starting with attacks on Communist infiltration routes at the Laotian northern end of the Ho Chi Minh Trail and culminating in a limited but progressively more intense campaign of bombing against North Vietnamese targets. Taylor now suggested that the proposed plan for this air campaign closely mirrored the March North land campaign proposed by Khanh, and could therefore be recommended to the South Vietnamese as a pair of synergistic campaigns so long as the South Vietnamese were prepared to make a major effort commensurate with the U.S. commitment. The U.S. could thus inform the South Vietnamese that it was investigating the possibility of exerting military pressure directly on North Vietnam, offering to implement the plan if South Vietnam began the reforms which had been needed for so long. Taylor claimed that his suggested course of action would promote the stability long wanted by the U.S. for South Vietnam, and would also convince the Communists that

ABOVE: South Vietnamese servicemen learn the intricacies of belt-fed machine guns on the outriggers of a Bell UH-1 Huey helicopter.

OPPOSITE: Montagnard commandos prepare for a patrol into Viet Cong territory at a Commando Training Center (Special Forces) in 1963.

continued aggression against South Vietnam would in fact visit destruction on themselves.

Johnson accepted the concept, but at this stage authorized no more than its first elements. Although the Americans would intensify air attacks against infiltration routes in Laos, and support South Vietnamese covert naval operations along the coast of North Vietnam, it would go no further. Johnson also authorized Taylor to tell the South Vietnamese that there was the possibility of joint U.S. and South Vietnamese air attacks on North Vietnam only as responses to Communist attacks in South Vietnam, but also that he should lay emphasis on the fact that such attacks would start only when the U.S. had evidence that the South Vietnamese had implemented the reforms which would allow them to cope with the almost inevitable escalation of the Communist effort in South Vietnam.

The level of operations authorized by Johnson were launched almost immediately after Taylor's return to South Vietnam, but neither the U.S. air attacks on Laos nor the South Vietnamese naval operations along North Vietnam's coast had any appreciable effect. The naval program had barely been launched before the onset of the monsoon season caused its termination.

The escalation of the air war over Laos started on December 14 with the launch of Operation Barrel Roll, which also failed as Johnson had limited the effort to a pair of missions, each with only four aircraft, each

The Gulf of Tonkin Incident

President Johnson's Speech to the American People on August 4, 1964. The Gulf of Tonkin Incident

On August 4, shortly before midnight in 1964, President Johnson made a television announcement in which he described an attack by North Vietnamese vessels on two US Navy warships, the *Maddox* and the *Turner Joy*. He then went on to inform the American people that a retaliatory attack was already in progress. He reiterated the firm commitment to both the American people, and the South Vietnamese government to secure peace in South Vietnam. He also reminded Americans that there was no desire for war and it was his solemn responsibility to order even limited action by American forces. The Gulf of Tonkin incident marked the beginning of major U.S. military intervention in the Vietnam War. (*See page 28*).

The Escalation of American Involvement in the Vietnam War

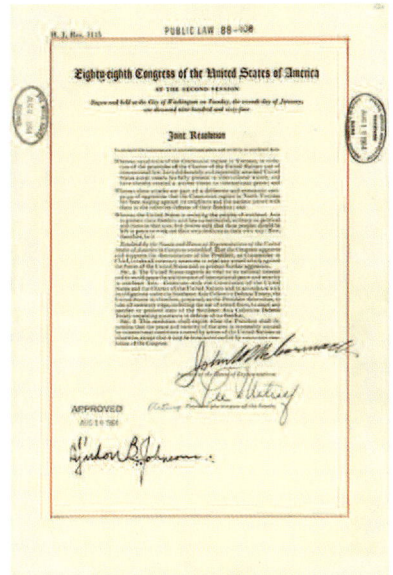

August 1964 crisis to draft a new constitution and pave the way to the establishment of a civilian government. Comprising of civilians of senior years, representing a broad cross-section of South Vietnamese society, the HNC met with universal indifference but nonetheless managed to get on the wrong side of Khanh, whose preoccupation was to ensure that a civilian government was little more than a respectable façade for continued military rule.

The HNC appointed an agricultural engineer of considerable years, Phan Khac Suu, as head of state, and Suu nominated a former schoolteacher and the current mayor of Saigon, Tran Van Huong, as prime minister. Progressing down the ladder of supposed power, Huong selected technicians rather than politicians as members of his cabinet, and in the process managed to alienate both the Buddhists and the Roman Catholics, each of whom demanded political power. Both religious groups were soon sponsoring street riots, but with Khanh's promise of military support, Huong declared martial law and managed to suppress the rioters; this merely worsened matters, Khanh being in no real position to support Huong as he himself was in deep political trouble. The "Young Turks," a group of young officers (so-called after the organization of young officers which dominated Turkish politics in 1908–18), had been among Huong's most important supporters, but were now becoming increasingly unhappy with Khanh. Air Vice Marshal Nguyen Cao Ky informed General William C. Westmoreland,

week. Adding insult to injury, moreover, Barrel Roll was so limited that the North Vietnamese did not even know it existed, and believed the attacks were just another aspect of the armed reconnaissance flights American warplanes were already making. Just as inevitably, the reforms to which Khanh had readily agreed were never implemented. Here the cause of the difficulty lay with the High National Council, a body established in the aftermath of the

ABOVE: The Gulf of Tonkin Resolution signed by President Lyndon B. Johnson.

RIGHT: Chart showing the U.S. Navy's interpretation of the events of the first part of the Gulf of Tonkin incident. It shows the track of the U.S. Navy destoyer USS *Maddox (DD-731)*, July 31–August 2, 1964, during the first part of the Gulf of Tonkin incident.

OVERLEAF: Australian soldiers on active duty in Vietnam.

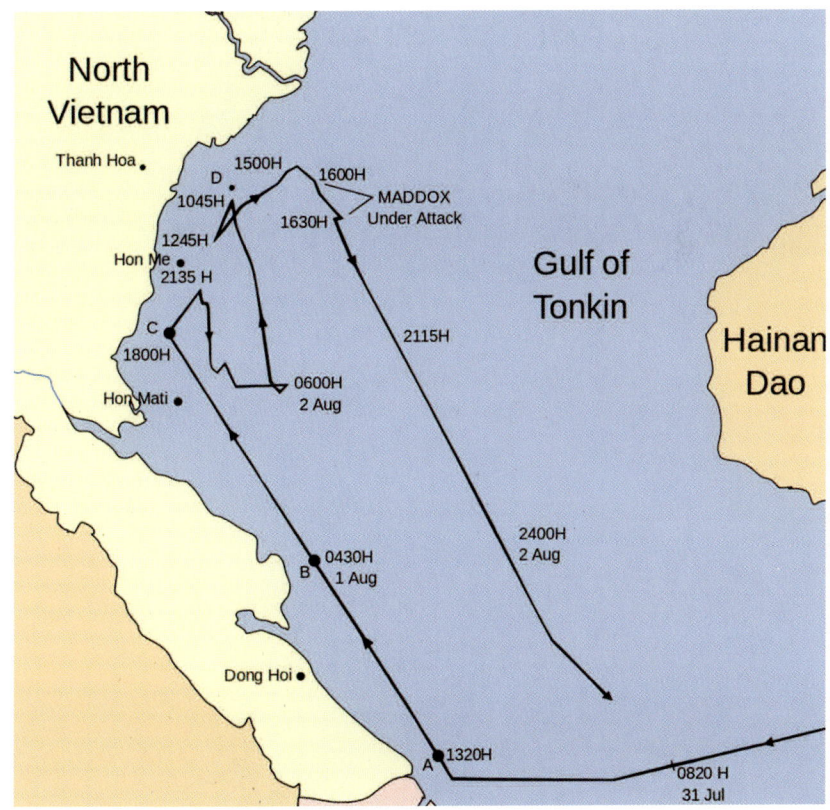

25

The Gulf of Tonkin Incident

The Escalation of American Involvement in the Vietnam War

The Gulf of Tonkin Incident

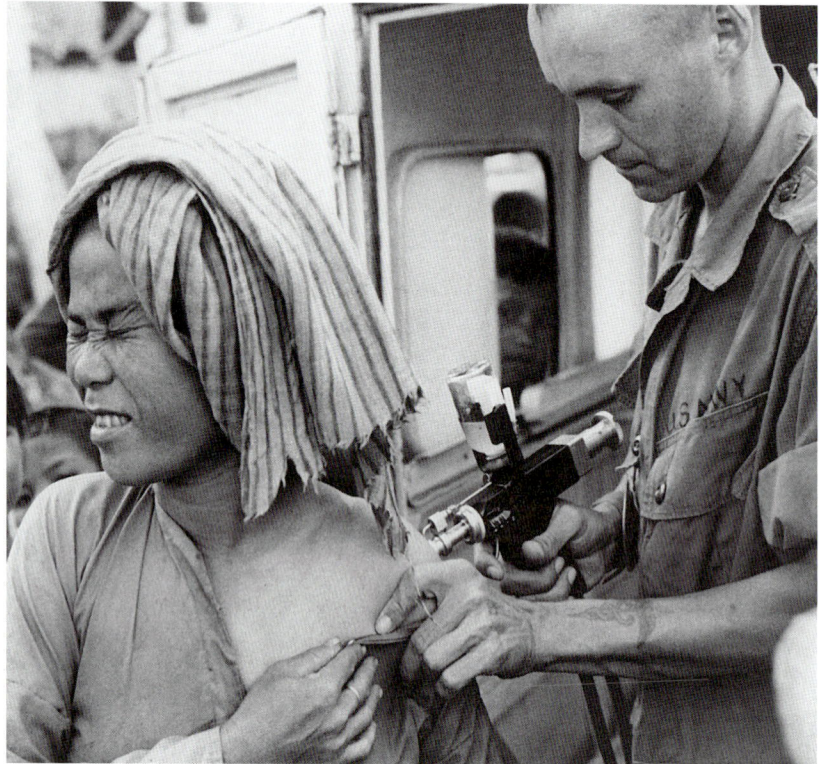

Lyndon Johnson–Report on the Gulf of Tonkin Incident

Harkin's successor as head of the MACV, that the combination of military setbacks in rural areas, Khanh's compromises with the Buddhists, and his continued refusal to act decisively, had persuaded the Young Turks that there had to be a change of leadership.

Very soon after this, therefore, senior officers of the South Vietnamese armed forces established an Armed Forces "aid" Khanh in military matters. A showdown was clearly in the immediate offing, so Taylor and Westmoreland arranged an informal meeting of the opposing factions to warn that continued disorder would create a strongly adverse effect on the U.S.'s relationship with South Vietnam. Only political stability, the Americans insisted, would ensure an increase in U.S. aid. The generals agreed to work together to promote this object but, as always in South Vietnamese politics, this was a mere fiction to buy time. In fact the time bought was very little, for on December 19 the Young Turks asked Khanh to remove the senior officers blocking the paths of their own promotions, by having the HNC mandate the retirement of all general officers with more than 25 years of service. Khanh agreed to do this, but the HNC refused and was thereupon dismissed, so triggering angry exchanges between Taylor, Khanh, and the Young Turks. Taylor saw that Khanh had effectively prevented any implementation of mutual military operations along the lines desired by the U.S. administration's action, and severely chastised Ky and others of the Young Turks, on the grounds that irresponsible actions of the officer corps had ended the possibility of military planning reliant on South Vietnamese stability.

On the following day, Taylor met Khanh and suggested that the latter should retire and leave the country. Khanh responded on December 22 with an obvious attempt to unify the officer corps behind him by invoking national honor: it was better, Khanh promulgated in an order of the day, "to live poor but proud as free citizens of an independent country than in ease and shame as slaves of the foreigners and Communists." In an interview with a correspondent of the *New York Herald Tribune*, Khanh claimed that Taylor had undertaken activities "beyond imagination as far as an ambassador is concerned."

LEFT: Using a modern means of injection, a member of one of the 21 U.S. military teams, under the Provincial Health Assistance Program (PHAP), inoculates an apprehensive Vietnamese woman against cholera. The PHAP program was co-ordinated, and in many cases financed, by the Agency for International Development (US AID) and currently maintains 43 U.S. and free-world medical teams in 43 provinces of South Vietnam.

OPPOSITE: U.S. soldiers surveying an area in Quang Tri province.

The Escalation of American Involvement in the Vietnam War

When Khanh's assertion appeared in print, the Department of State backed Taylor, confirming that the ambassador had acted with the full support of the U.S. government. Secretary of State Dean Rusk began the process of checking the Young Turks by stating that the U.S. would soon end some of its assistance to South Vietnam as the Khanh administration was clearly not prepared to use the aid properly.

In a terrorist attack of great audacity on December 24, the Viet Cong bombed the Brink Hotel in Saigon, where many U.S. officers were billeted. The attack killed two Americans and injured 51 U.S. and South Vietnamese citizens. This was the type of event which should have triggered joint U.S. and South Vietnamese action but, against Taylor's advice, Johnson now refused to authorize air attacks on North Vietnam. In this refusal, Johnson was acting in the belief that without indisputable evidence of the Viet Cong's responsibility for the bombing, the U.S. people might construe the attack as provocation engineered by Khanh. Johnson also hoped that the Young Turks might draw the conclusion that the lack of retaliation

The Gulf of Tonkin Incident

The Escalation of American Involvement in the Vietnam War

OPPOSITE: Sgt. 1st Class Robert Daniel, a heavy weapons non-commissioned officer of Detachment A730, 7th Special Forces, gives instruction on the workings of the 60-mm mortar to trainees of the Civil Irregular Defense Group in Thua Thien, in 1963.

ABOVE: The M113 Armored Personnel Carrier added a new dimension of mobility to the Vietnamese theater of war, in that it was amphibious.

was the result of their own performance in the periods just past, and so decide to eschew factionalism in favor of a united national resistance to Communism.

Johnson's thinking seems to have been right. Over the next ten days, the U.S. embassy, Khanh, and the Young Turks achieved a compromise which returned Huong and a civilian government to office, even though it did not restore the HNC. But the compromise had no effect on the task

of restoring order in South Vietnam. The **Buddhists** were already sworn to oppose any regime headed by Huong and, on his return to office, began to look for a reason to remove him. Such a pretext arrived on January 17, 1965, when Huong decreed an enlargement of the national draft for the South Vietnamese forces. Buddhist agitators were almost immediately out on the streets preaching rebellion, civil unrest spread to every major urban center in South Vietnam, the 8,000-book U.S.

The Gulf of Tonkin Incident

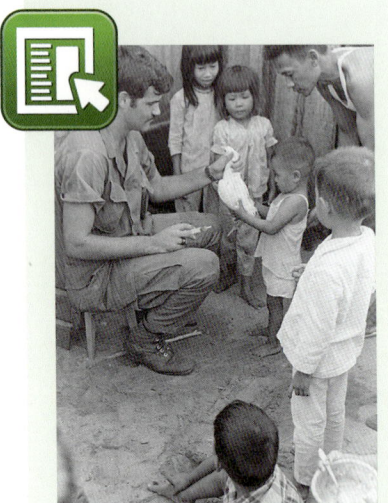

Operation Helping Hand was a program conducted almost entirely by volunteers, with funds primarily supplied from voluntary contributions. It consisted of building adequate houses for men of the Vietnamese navy and their dependents and teaching the Vietnamese how to raise chickens, pigs, and ducks and to make the most of the fishing available. Here, the Vietnamese are being trained in the proper care and feeding of livestock. New breeds were also introduced in the hope of providing them with a future as well as an immediate relief to their food problem.

Information Agency Library in Hue was destroyed, and a teenage girl burned herself to death in the first example of self-immolation since the anti-Diem rioting more than 12 months earlier. On January 27, the Young Turks, bent on action, launched a coup, declared that Huong was not capable of maintaining order, and demanded that Khanh form a new government.

Against the background of political turmoil in Saigon and South Vietnam's other major cities, fighting continued in the rural area around the capital, and here the Viet Cong inexorably gained the upper hand. During the last week of December 1964, for example, Communist forces occupied the village of Binh Gia (in Phuoc Tuy province), an anti-Communist community of 6,000 people located on the coast near Saigon. The subsequent Battle of Binh Gia, which was only part of a larger Communist undertaking, was fought between December 28, 1964 and January 1, 1965; not only did it mark a signal defeat for the South Vietnamese army but it also provided striking evidence of the problem facing the USA as it struggled to find ways of propping up the South Vietnamese regime.

BELOW: A U.S. adviser, working with children in Vietnam in August 1964.

OPPOSITE: Casualties of war: Vietnamese orphans onboard a U.S. ship.

Toward the close of 1964, the fact that South Vietnam was facing political instability in the aftermath of the coup against Diem presented the Communists with the ideal opportunity to exploit the South Vietnamese government's adverse political and military situation, and at the same time pursue instructions from North Vietnam to start a program of military offensives. Within this overall situation, the National Liberation Front seized the opportunity to commemorate the fourth anniversary of its establishment

The Escalation of American Involvement in the Vietnam War

with a major military victory. The first operational formation of the Viet Cong, the 9th Viet Cong Division, was entrusted with the task, and in many respects far exceeded the hopes which had been placed on it. Thus the fighting in and around Binh Gia demonstrated that the Communist forces in South Vietnam had reached the level of military maturity at which they could commit themselves to combat with equanimity against the best South Vietnamese army formations.

On October 11, 1964 the senior political and military leadership in North Vietnam had ordered the NLF to carry out a series of offensives during the winter and spring of 1965. To help the southern insurgents carry out their offensive, General Nguyen Chi Thanh was nominated to supervise the full range of military operations in South Vietnam, while officers such as Major General Le Trong Tan were responsible for military preparations, which began during November. As part of the operation, the Nam Bo Regional Command identified its key areas of operations as the Baria-Long Khanh and the Binh Long-Phuoc Long regions. The 271st and 272nd Viet Cong Regiments were selected for the forthcoming operation and were placed under the command of the Forward Command Committee. Having completed their training, thay began to move in the direction of the Baria-Long Khanh region. With North Vietnamese assistance, the Viet Cong built up their stocks of weapons, ammunition and other vital matériel, and were instructed to destroy any South Vietnamese army units along Routes 2 and 15.

In the first days of November 1964, the 271st and 272nd Viet Cong

The Gulf of Tonkin Incident

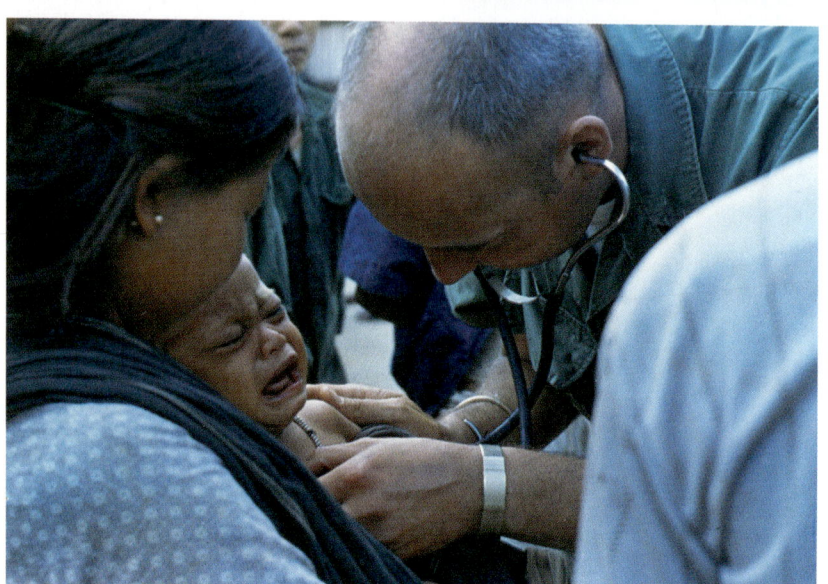

ABOVE & LEFT: A US Medical Civic Action Program (MEDCAP) team from the sub-sector, III Corps, MACV, treated 624 patients from the island village of Thai Hung, 9 miles (15km) north-west of Bien Hoa on the Saigon river. Pfc. Marcelino Galvin (right), 25th Medical Battalion, 173rd Airborne Brigade Infantry Division, dispenses medicine to a villager who has been seen by the doctor. October 1966.

Regiments, supported by the 80th Viet Cong Artillery Detachment, moved out of War Zone D, and by the end of the month had reached their rendezvous location, where they were joined by the 500th and 800th Viet

The Escalation of American Involvement in the Vietnam War

BELOW: While the talks in Paris between the North and South Vietnamese delegates were stopped, following the announcement of the death of President Ho Chi Minh of North Vietnam, war was still raging in South Vietnam between the Americans and Viet Cong forces. Meanwhile, members of the Viet Cong continued to transport arms and ammunitions to soldiers through the thick forests and mountains of South Vietnam.

Cong Battalions from Military Region 7, the 186th Viet Cong Battalion from Military Region 6, and the 445th Viet Cong Company from the Hoai Duc district.

Before committing themselves to the main phase of the operation, the Viet Cong inflicted many casualties on South Vietnamese forces in five separate engagements, the South Vietnamese army losing two first-line and one reserve battalions. An entire company of South Vietnamese M113 Armored Personnel Carriers was also destroyed on December 9, which allowed the Viet Cong to overrun the Hoai Duc district and several strategic hamlets such as Dat Do, Long Thanh and Nhon Trach.

By a time early in January 1965 the Viet Cong had significantly enlarged its theater of operations, and the Communists were planning more military operations against major South Vietnamese installations, with Binh Gia the next target. This village was surrounded by rubber and banana plantations, and was located about 42 miles (67km) from Saigon. Most of the inhabitants were Roman Catholics fleeing from North Vietnam as a result of Communist persecution, and the local priest was the commander of the militia forces.

The Gulf of Tonkin Incident

The 9th Viet Cong Division, with the 514th Viet Cong Battalion in the lead, began its assault during the early morning of December 28, quickly overrunning several outposts and overwhelming the local militia forces without difficulty. Later in the morning of the same day, two South Vietnamese Ranger units attempted a counterattack, but were unable to clear the Viet Cong from their positions, although they did briefly reach a point only 330 yards (300m) from Binh Gia village before a Viet Cong battalion drove them back. Reinforcements from the 30th and 33rd Rangers arrived on the following day but could not dislodge the Viet Cong, which was now well dug-in; after some heavy fighting the Ranger battalions were heavily damaged by Viet Cong machine gun fire. On the morning of December 30, the South Vietnamese 4th Marine Battalion was delivered by helicopter, recapturing Binh Gia without difficulty as the Viet Cong had disappeared; but later on the same day a U.S. Army gunship was shot down, and all four of the crew were killed.

One company of the 4th Marine Battalion was sent to the crash site to recover the bodies, but once again the South Vietnamese were ambushed and pinned down. On the morning of December 31, the rest of 4th Marine Battalion was committed in an attempt to rescue the trapped company. At the site of the crash, the 4th Marine Battalion and its U.S. advisers located fresh graves, which turned out to be a ploy for another ambush in which the Viet Cong launched strong attacks. Further South Vietnamese reinforcements, of

LEFT: American and allied soldiers during the defense of Saigon.

The Gulf of Tonkin Incident

the 29th, 30th, and 33rd Ranger Battalions, were ambushed and took heavy losses. This latest stage of the battle led to the death of 35 South Vietnamese officers, 112 Marines, and 71 wounded, bringing the total casualties to more than 300; six U.S. advisers were also killed. On January 1 more South Vietnamese reinforcements arrived, but they were too late.

Despite the fact that it had been heavily defeated, the South Vietnamese army stubbornly asserted that it had won a victory, the Viet Cong being no longer in Binh Gia. The battle had nonetheless provided striking evidence of the Viet Cong's growing military strength, especially in the region of the Mekong river delta. This was the first occasion on which the National Liberation Front had undertaken a large-scale operation, holding its ground and fighting for four days against government troops supported by armor, artillery, and helicopters. The Viet Cong had demonstrated that with the aid of weapons and supplies from North Vietnam it could fight and defeat the best units the South Vietnamese army possessed. In recognition of the regiment's performance during the Binh Gia campaign, the NLF high command bestowed the honor title "Binh Gia Regiment" on the 271st Viet Cong. After the campaign, all the Viet Cong units involved withdrew to War Zone D in order to plan the next offensive, which was to be directed against Dong Xoai.

This was an event of great significance, for it persuaded Westmoreland that the Communist forces were trying out new tactics, possibly with a view to making the switch from irregular and small unit warfare to a more conventional conflict in which large units attacked to take and then hold ground. Westmoreland and Taylor agreed that in the hope of prompting a new sense of unity in the South Vietnamese, the

LEFT: A grenade-type booby trap, used by the CIDG at the Tran Sup checkpoint, about 5 miles (8km) north-west of Tay Ninh City. November 1966.

OPPOSITE: In addition to normal combat operations while on a combined sweep operation in Binh Duong province in September 1965, approximately 20 miles (32km) north of Saigon, elements of the 173rd Airborne Brigade conduct civic action and psychological warfare activities. Sgt. Arnold S. Jaudon, 172nd Missile Battalion, hands leaflets to be stored on the aircraft until drop time to 1st Lt. James R. Paris, U.S. Army Broadcast and Visual Activities, Pacific, who is on temporary duty to Military Assistance Command, Vietnam (MACV).

The Escalation of American Involvement in the Vietnam War

U.S. should respond in a fashion it had not yet tried, and therefore recommended to Johnson that the bombing of North Vietnam should be commenced. Assistant Secretary of State William P. Bundy concurred with the suggestion of Westmoreland and Taylor, claiming that the Binh Gia setback indicated a new low in South Vietnam's already heavily compromised national morale. All that was required, everyone agreed, was for the North Vietnamese to provide the right kind of provocation.

Text-Dependent Questions

1. What report led to speculation that the second attack in the Gulf of Tonkin incident did not happen?

2. What two U.S. Navy destroyers were involved in the Gulf of Tonkin incident?

3. What was *Operation Helping Hand*?

Research Projects

What evidence is there to suggest that the Gulf of Tonkin incident may not have happened exactly as reported at the time.

VIETNAM WAR

Chapter Two
"ROLLING THUNDER"

The provocation for which the Johnson administration has been waiting was duly delivered on February 7, 1965, when the Viet Cong attacked the compound and associated airstrip of the U.S. advisory team at Camp Holloway, near Pleiku in the Central Highlands, killing nine Americans and wounding more than 100. Following on almost immediately from the "Tet Truce," an unofficial cease-fire by the Viet Cong from February 1–6 to mark the start of the Vietnamese New Year, the attack seemed to be a deliberate provocation,

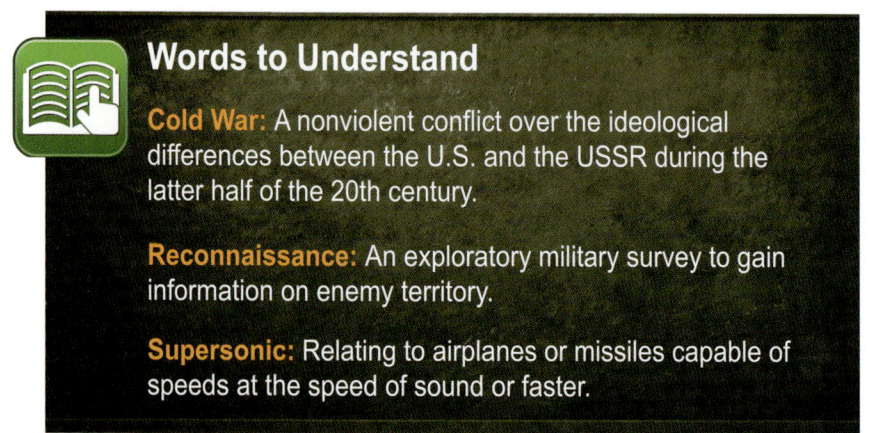

Words to Understand

Cold War: A nonviolent conflict over the ideological differences between the U.S. and the USSR during the latter half of the 20th century.

Reconnaissance: An exploratory military survey to gain information on enemy territory.

Supersonic: Relating to airplanes or missiles capable of speeds at the speed of sound or faster.

possibly designed to impress the Soviet premier, Alexei Kosygin, who was then in Hanoi on an official visit.

The leader of a U.S. observation mission in Saigon at this time was McGeorge Bundy, the National Security adviser, who recommended an immediate retaliatory raid on North Vietnam. Johnson concurred, and on the very same day 49 warplanes of the U.S. Navy attacked the Communist barracks at Dong Hoi just to the north of the DMZ, a target specifically selected so as to offer no threat to Kosygin. Delayed by inclement weather until the following day, the South Vietnamese component of the attack struck another barracks at Vinh, in the same area.

Johnson told the USA: "We have no choice now but to clear the decks, and make absolutely clear our continued determination to back South Vietnam in its fight to maintain its independence." Soon after this, Taylor recommended to Johnson the beginning of a "measured, controlled sequence of actions" against North Vietnam, a sentiment with which Bundy agreed.

The Viet Cong struck again on February 10, this time in Qui Nhon, destroying a hotel used as a billet for U.S. enlisted personnel and killing 23 men as the building collapsed. Many other men were trapped and injured in the rubble. Johnson now authorized a second series of reprisals, and two days later announced that Operation Rolling Thunder would be launched as a "measured and limited air action" against military targets in the regions of North Vietnam to the south of the 19th parallel.

The first series of air attacks following the Communist offensives on Pleiku and Qui Nhon were Operations Flaming Dart I and Faming Dart II. The attacks had originally been conceived as part of a

OPPOSITE: Two airborne U.S. Navy Douglas A-4 Skyhawk light bombers in the skies above Vietnam in Feb 1967.

RIGHT: Members of the Vietnam People's Army prepare to ward off a U.S. air attack.

"Rolling Thunder"

The Escalation of American Involvement in the Vietnam War

OPPOSITE: The aircraft carrier CVAN-65 (USS *Enterprise*), equipped with Douglas A-4C Skyhawks, at sea off Vietnam.

ABOVE: A Vought F-8 Crusader shot down in North Vietnam.

three-phase "program" that had begun with the Operation Barrel Roll air attacks on Communist targets inside Laos during December 1964, and had therefore already been planned. A total of 49 sorties was flown for Flaming Dart I on February 7, and 99 sorties for Flaming Dart II on February 11, the first targeting North Vietnamese army bases near Dong Hoi, and the second Viet Cong logistics and communications facilities near the DMZ.

The U.S. reaction to the perceived Communist escalation was not limited to attacks on targets in North Vietnam. The Johnson administration also allowed the use of U.S. warplanes to tackle Communist targets in South Vietnam. On February 19 Martin B-57 twin-jet bombers of the USAF undertook the first attacks flown by the U.S. forces in jet-powered aircraft, rather than piston-engined machines such as the Douglas A-1 Skyraider and Douglas B-26 Invader, in support of South Vietnamese ground units. On February 24 jet-powered warplanes of the USAF were used again over South Vietnam, in this instance to destroy a Communist ambush in the Central Highlands by means of a massive series of tactical air sorties.

The first mission of the Rolling Thunder campaign was scheduled for February 20 but was canceled, together with its immediate successors, after an attempted coup in Saigon, which caused the final overthrow of Khanh as Phan Huy Quat, a civilian, became the nominal prime minister as a front for continued military rule. Rolling Thunder was finally launched on March 2, when U.S. and South Vietnamese warplanes destroyed an

43

"Rolling Thunder"

The Escalation of American Involvement in the Vietnam War

USA launches Operation Rolling Thunder in Vietnam

ammunition depot and a naval base in North Vietnam. This was a week after the U.S. administration made the first official announcement that U.S. airmen were flying combat missions against the Viet Cong.

Rolling Thunder was planned as a graduated campaign in which any concessions by the Communists would result in a scaling-back of the air operation, but was a failure inasmuch as it appears to have had no significant material effect, and in fact probably hardened the resolve of the North Vietnamese and their South Vietnamese adherents to tightening the screw, Rolling Thunder having made little apparent impact by holding true to its overall plan. Part of this failure to make an immediate impact resulted from Johnson's refusal to allow more than two to four raids, by only modest numbers of warplanes, each week. Westmoreland believed, probably correctly, that this was a tactic which hardly suggested any real resolve in U.S. planning, caused only insignificant damage, and at the same time added risk but not results to the U.S. position vis-à-vis the Vietnam War. The North Vietnamese response was the exploitation of its links with

LEFT: An F-8 Crusader on the aircraft carrier CVA-64 (USS *Constellation*).

45

"Rolling Thunder"

the Chinese and Soviets to undertake, as a matter of great urgency, the construction of a comprehensive air-defense system of the Soviet pattern, with radar and observer sites feeding data to a central headquarters which exercised tight control of antiaircraft artillery, surface-to-air missiles, and fighters. Westmoreland had stated, quite prophetically, that Rolling Thunder would "result in mounting casualties as the war goes on – perhaps more than we are willing or even able to sustain."

Rolling Thunder was thus a sustained and graduated campaign by the U.S. Air Force's 2nd Air Division (later the 7th Air Force), the U.S. Navy, and South Vietnamese air forces against targets in North Vietnam to November 1, 1968. The operation's four objectives, which had not been fixed at the beginning of the campaign and evolved during the period in which they were undertaken, were to bolster the morale and resolve of the South Vietnamese government;

LEFT: Three armed Vietnamese women. To resist the U.S. Air Force bombing over North Vietnam between the 17th and 19th parallels, the inhabitants of the Quang Trach district in Quang Binh province constructed 60 miles (100km) of trenches, leading from each house to the center of the village.

OPPOSITE: Bombs from U.S. aircraft strike their targets in North Vietnam. Operation Rolling Thunder was designed to inflict major damage on North Vietnam's physical infrastructure and convince the North Vietnamese of America's determination not to allow the defeat of South Vietnam. But the campaign was fought at too low a level and in too desultory a fashion to achieve its objectives.

provide the North Vietnamese government with strong evidence of the futility of supporting Communist insurgency in South Vietnam; eliminate North Vietnam's transportation and communications networks, industrial base, and air-defense system; and to curtail if not halt the movement of men and matériel from North Vietnam to South Vietnam. The implementation of this entire scheme would have been difficult under the most benign of operating conditions, and within the context of a totally free military hand, but was in fact rendered difficult if not impossible by the political and military limitations imposed on the U.S. and South Vietnamese air forces, and by the extensive nature of the military aid which North Vietnam received from the USSR and China.

The operation was the most intensive air campaign undertaken in the course of the "Cold War" period, and also the most problematical undertaken by the U.S. air forces since the U.S. Army Air Force's daylight bombing campaign against Germany in the Second World War. With the aid of its Communist supporters in China and the USSR, the North Vietnamese were able to construct a complex and multi-layered air-defense system, using air-to-air as well as surface-to-air weapons, and this posed U.S. airmen with some of the most difficult tactical problems they had ever encountered.

By the end of August of the previous year, in their follow-up to the Gulf of Tonkin Resolution, the Joint Chiefs of Staff had drawn up a list of 94 targets to be destroyed as part of a coordinated eight-week air campaign against North Vietnam's transportation network, and within this context bridges, railway marshalling yards, docks, barracks, and supply dumps were to be attacked and destroyed. Johnson was concerned that the U.S. campaign might spark a direct intervention by the Chinese or Soviets, which might escalate into a world war. With the support of McNamara, Johnson refused to authorize a bombing campaign that was so extensive in its targeting aims, and it was this which limited the scope of the Flaming Dart operations, which followed the Communist attacks on U.S. personnel at Pleiku and Qui Nhon, to hit targets in the southern region of North Vietnam, where most of the North Vietnamese army and its supply dumps were located.

Then, after coming under considerable pressure from the Joint Chiefs of Staff as the Communist forces continued to gain success after success in South Vietnam, Johnson gave his approval to Rolling Thunder as a sustained bombing effort to be linked directly to any overt Communist activities. Rolling Thunder was initially to have been an eight-week campaign wholly consistent with the restrictions imposed by Johnson and McNamara, but if the Communist military operations in South Vietnam were "with DRV [Democratic Republic of

"Rolling Thunder"

Vietnam] support, strikes against the DRV would be extended with intensified efforts against targets north of the 19th parallel." The Johnson administration believed that the combination of carefully controlled military and diplomatic pressure would persuade North Vietnam to call off its campaign in South Vietnam. The U.S. military machine was not as optimistic, as the campaign as currently envisaged was limited to the region south of the 19th parallel, and even then the targets had to be approved on an individual basis by Johnson and McNamara.

On March 2, the first mission of the Rolling Thunder campaign was flown against an ammunition storage dump in the area of Xom Bang, and on the same date South Vietnamese Skyraider warplanes attacked the naval base at Quang Khe. This first effort came as a very rude shock to the Americans, however, for they lost six aircraft shot down. Although five of the downed aircrew were rescued, it was clear from this very first stage that the U.S. was not going to have it all its own way.

In accordance with the idea of graduated response, whereby the threat of next-step destruction was supposed to signal U.S. determination more strongly than the destruction itself, it was deemed more beneficial to U.S. intentions to hold important targets under constant threat by bombing those of lesser importance. From the very start of Rolling Thunder, these were decided by senior political and military figures in the USA, who set not only the targets to be attacked, but also even the tactical details, such as the time of the attack on the given day, the number and types of warplanes to be flown, the tonnages and types of ordnance to be used, and, on occasion, even the direction of the attack. Attacks were forbidden within 34.5 miles (55.5km) of Hanoi and 12.5 miles (20km) of Haiphong, and a buffer zone 34.5 miles (55.5km) wide extended along the North Vietnamese/Chinese frontier. Many have since demonstrated that the allocation of targets bore no relationship to the realities of the military situation, and that the approval of targets was made on a random and even illogical basis. An obvious target type for initial attack, namely the airfields of North Vietnam, was also on the list of prohibited targets. These prohibitions were later interpreted more loosely or even removed, but the administration nonetheless exercised a very real control over the bombing on a day-to-day basis, with very adverse effects on the overall success of the campaign, as those in Washington could not be in full command of the situation in South-East Asia.

48

The Escalation of American Involvement in the Vietnam War

OPPOSITE: Pilots of Air Squadron 2 of the Vietnam People's Air Force, ready to take off in their Russian-made MiG-21s. 1968.

ABOVE: U.S. airmen kit themselves up for a mission.

One of the campaign's primary objectives, as far as the military professionals were concerned, should have been Haiphong and other North Vietnamese ports, which could have been mined to halt, or at least delay, the arrival of weapons and other matériel by sea from other Communist countries. Johnson felt this might be too great a provocation for the USSR and China to stomach, however, and it was only in 1972, when it was too late to affect the outcome of the war, that aerial mining of this type was finally permitted. There was almost no liaison between Johnson and his senior military officers in Washington with regard to the matter of selecting targets for Rolling Thunder: even the chairman of the Joint Chiefs of Staff, General Earl G. Wheeler of the U.S. Army, was not present for most of the critical discussions of 1965, and this was also true of the process in its later years.

Most of the Rolling Thunder attacks were launched from a quarter of Thai air bases, namely Korat, Takhli, Udon Thani, and Ubon. After taking off and heading toward North Vietnam, the attacking warplanes generally refueled in the air over Laos before entering North Vietnamese air space. After attacking their targets, the process generally being a shallow dive-bombing maneuver, the warplanes then either returned directly to their Thai bases or departed over the relatively safe waters of the Gulf of Tonkin. Operational experience soon suggested that a system of routing was required to reduce the chances of air space conflict between USAF aircraft, arriving from the direction of Thailand, and U.S. Navy/U.S. Marine Corps aircraft making their entry from the Gulf of Tonkin, so the U.S. planners divided North Vietnam into six target regions designated as "route packages," and each of these was allocated to the USAF or U.S. Navy/U.S. Marine Corps, the aircraft of one service being strongly prohibited from entering any route package allocated to the other.

The attacks undertaken by aircraft of the U.S. Navy and U.S. Marine Corps were launched from the aircraft carriers of Task Force 77, cruising off the coast of North Vietnam on the so-called "Yankee Station." The naval and marine aircraft, which generally carried a lighter bomb load and had shorter range than their land-based

49

"Rolling Thunder"

counterparts of the USAF, were allocated the route packages that allowed them to approach their targets directly from seaward, and the very considerable majority of the attacks launched from aircraft carriers were therefore directed on targets in the coastal area of North Vietnam.

On April 3 the Joint Chiefs of Staff persuaded Johnson and McNamara that there was every reason to suppose that a sustained campaign, lasting four weeks, against North Vietnam's communications network, in the widest sense of that term, would yield a handsome operational dividend in isolating North Vietnam from the receipt of all but insignificant quantities of supplies from the USSR and China, and would also prevent the distribution of any supplies within North Vietnam and thence to the Communist forces in South Vietnam via the Ho Chi Minh Trail. The Joint Chiefs of Staff indicated that about 33 percent of North Vietnam's imports arrived in the country along the north-east railway from China, and the other 67 percent by sea through Haiphong and North Vietnam's other eastern ports. Their recommendation was therefore based, for the first time in the campaign, on the selection of targets on the basis of their military importance rather than their psychological significance as modified for political and diplomatic reasons.

Johnson and McNamara accepted the recommendation of the Joint Chiefs of Staff, and during the resulting four-week campaign 26 bridges and seven ferries were destroyed; other militarily important targets attacked during the same periods included North Vietnam's already large ground-based search and fire-control radar system, barracks, depots for ammunition, and other military supplies.

LEFT: A U.S. pilot, captured by the North Vietnamese, has his injuries attended to by a Vietnamese woman.

OPPOSITE ABOVE: Diving down on a military target in North Vietnam, the pilot of a USAF F-105 Thunderchief fires a volley of 70-mm (2.75 inch) rockets. The Thunderchief is also equipped with 100-shot-per-second Vulcan automatic cannons for strafing.

OPPOSITE BELOW: USAF personnel of the 435th Munitions Maintenance Squadron hurriedly pull the chocks away from an armed F-100 Super Sabre, ready for take-off from the Phan Rang airbase in South Vietnam.

The Escalation of American Involvement in the Vietnam War

control from Washington was a process of extreme complication and inflexibility when attacks on fixed targets had to be requested, selected, and finally authorized.

Rolling Thunder was conceived as the means to indicate to North Vietnam the determination of the USA to prevent a Communist takeover of South Vietnam, but signally failed in this objective, for North Vietnam persevered in its sponsorship and involvement in the war in South Vietnam. When the U.S. suggested peace talks to North Vietnam on April 8, the latter's government replied that it would only consider such an undertaking after the U.S. bombing attacks had been called off, the U.S. had removed all its forces from South Vietnam, the South Vietnamese administration recognized the demands of the NLF, and there was general agreement that all matters

Throughout the period, it was the panhandle southern region of North Vietnam which was still the primary focus of the air attacks, and the number of sorties flown over the region increased from a figure of 3,600 in April to 4,000 in May. Also of note during this period, moreover, was a slow switch from attacks on fixed targets to operations deemed to be of the "armed reconnaissance" type. In this latter, small groups of warplanes overflew roads, railways, rivers, and canals, constantly on the look-out for targets of opportunity. Sorties of this type had grown from two to 200 per week by the end of 1965, and the continuing nature of this effort, which yielded very useful results, meant that late in the Rolling Thunder campaign armed reconnaissance sorties amounted to some 75 percent of the bombing effort. The growth of the armed reconnaissance mission in part reflected its success, and in part the growing realization that tight

51

"Rolling Thunder"

pertaining to the reunification of the two Vietnams be negotiated by the Vietnamese themselves, without representation by any external power. This counter to the U.S. suggestion was nothing less than a robust rejection of the U.S.'s overture, and came a mere five days after the North Vietnamese air force was first encountered by American warplanes in the skies over North Vietnam. During this first aerial encounter, U.S.

ABOVE: Douglas B-66 Destroyer bombers prepared for action at Takhli Royal Thai Air Force Base in Thailand.

RIGHT: December 1968: USAF F-105 Thunderchiefs on a Combat Sky Spot mission.

aircraft came under attack by Mikoyan-Guryevich MiG-15 fighters, which were jet-powered machines supplied by the USSR. These were technically obsolescent warplanes, as quickly appreciated by the Americans, but were being flown with increasing levels of tactical skill and would in time pave the way for the introduction of more capable aircraft.

The entire nature of the U.S. commitment to South Vietnam changed radically and irrevocably on March 8, 1965, the date on which some 3,500 men of the U.S. Marine Corps landed on the beach at Da Nang, on the northern coast of South Vietnam. It was claimed at the time that the arrival of this force was designed to provide protection for the South Vietnamese airfields involved in the Rolling Thunder campaign, but the task of the newly-arrived force very soon changed from a defensive to an offensive nature as the Marines extended their patrol activities and began to search for Communist forces to tackle in combat. From this time onward the air campaign, which had been seen as the key to persuading North Vietnam to call off it efforts in South Vietnam, steadily became secondary to a growing land campaign in which the USA used the U.S. Marine Corps and U.S. Army in an

ABOVE: The much criticized bombing raids in North Vietnam by U.S. aircraft to smash the Communist supply routes nevertheless continued with stepped-up intensity, the initial spasmodic raids superseded by daily bombing sorties by multi-squadron formations. Apart from the raids hindering the supply of war materiél to the Communist troops, some observers believed it would place the U.S. and its allies in a better bargaining position if a peace conference were to take place.

attempt to secure military victory over the Communist forces operating in South Vietnam. U.S. ground troops were pouring into South Vietnam in ever-increasing numbers, and both the extent and intensity of the ground war was escalating rapidly.

Into the third week of April, the supposedly strategic air attacks of the Rolling Thunder campaign over North Vietnam had at least achieved parity with the tactical air operations flown over South Vietnam, but from this time onward the tactical air operations had the greater priority, and attacks on North Vietnamese targets, which interfered with the tactical air war over South Vietnam, were curtailed or even canceled.

By December 24, 1965, the balance of success and failure in Rolling Thunder was based on the loss of 180 U.S. aircraft (85, 94, and one, by the USAF, U.S. Navy, and U.S. Marine Corps respectively), while the North Vietnamese air force had lost eight fighters. The men of the USAF had flown 25,971 sorties and dropped 32,063 tons of bombs, while U.S. Navy and U.S. Marine Corps crews had made 28,168 sorties and dropped 11,144 tons of bombs; the South Vietnamese air force, meanwhile, had flown 682 missions to deliver an unrecorded tonnage of bombs.

The planners and commanders of the America's air forces also became highly concerned after April 5, 1966, when the interpretation of photographs taken by U.S. reconnaissance aircraft indicated that the North Vietnamese were building the types of sites associated only with the basing of surface-to-air missile batteries. The USAF and U.S. Navy then approached the authorities in Washington jointly, for authorization to attack and destroy these sites before the missiles for which they were intended could reach operational status, but were turned down on the basis that the majority of the sites in question lay near to if not actually inside the urban areas which political considerations had placed off-limits for U.S. air attack. Thus it was no great surprise to the U.S. military when a Republic F-105 Thunderchief

"Rolling Thunder"

attack warplane was brought down by an SA-2 "Guideline" missile on July 24. This event at least served to focus the minds of those in Washington on a major shift in the balance of the air war, and three days later permission was granted, albeit on a one-time basis, for an attack on the two missile sites believed to have been involved in the episode. Adding insult to injury, the U.S. attack then flew into a North Vietnamese trap, the two "missile sites" being dummy installations; while trying to tackle them the American pilots had been flying their warplanes into a concealed nest of radar-directed antiaircraft guns around the sites, as a result of which six U.S. aircraft were shot down, with two pilots killed, one declared missing, two captured and one taken captive.

On June 29, 1966, Johnson authorized attacks on North Vietnam's petroleum, oil, and lubricant storage areas. This was the type of operational-level target which the military had wanted to attack right from the start of the campaign, on the grounds that the loss of all its POL facilities would strike at the very heart of North Vietnam's ability to sustain the Communist forces in South Vietnam. The first attacks on these newly-authorized targets seemed to indicate a major success as they destroyed the facilities near Hanoi and Haiphong, the CIA then estimating that North Vietnam had lost 70 percent of its POL facilities, although the U.S. had also suffered heavily in the form of 43 aircraft which failed to return. North Vietnam, however, was

ABOVE: A bridge in North Vietnam, extensively damaged by USAF bombers.

OPPOSITE: A USAF Douglas A-1 Skyraider over South Vietnam in 1966.

not as reliant on oil products as the U.S. believed, and had also appreciated the fact that the U.S. might attack its major facilities. The North Vietnamese government had therefore arranged the dispersion, right across the country and in large numbers of individually small caches, of most of the country's POL stocks in drums. The U.S. attacks on North Vietnam's POL facilities were terminated on September 4 after U.S. intelligence resources admitted the

The Escalation of American Involvement in the Vietnam War

attacks had had little if any effect on North Vietnam's ability to sustain its war effort. North Vietnam was making greater use of coal to power its industries than the Americans had been prepared to concede and, in combination with draught animal and human power, the currently available POL stocks were adequate to the task.

The Rolling Thunder campaign also revealed many problems with the U.S. forces involved, and had an adverse effect on its other forces. A major difficulty, and one which found no solution until 1968, was command and control of the air effort in the whole of South-East Asia. While the USAF's 2nd Air Division, which was succeeded by the 7th Air Force on April 1, 1966, was nominally responsible for air operations over North and South Vietnam, it was actually the Air Component Command of the Military Assistance Command Vietnam, and it was the belief of Westmoreland, the MACV's commander, that the war would have to be won inside South Vietnam. The 7th/13th Air Force, based in Thailand and thus the origin of most of the USAF's heavier attacks on North Vietnam, had twin command structures, reporting to the 7th Air Force on operational matters and to the 13th Air Force, headquartered in the Philippine Islands, on logists and administration. This complex command and control factor became still more difficult after the division of the air campaign into four competing operational areas in South Vietnam, North Vietnam, and Laos (north and south). The U.S. Navy's Task Force 77 received its instructions via 7th Fleet from the commander-in-chief Pacific, a naval officer based in the Hawaiian Islands, via one of his subordinates, the USAF commander of the Pacific Air Forces.

Inter-service rivalries were also an interference, to a certain extent at least, in the smooth planning and conduct of air operations. The U.S. Navy was not readily prepared to see the full integration of its air activities over North Vietnam with those of the USAF. General William Momyer, commanding the 7th Air Force, had the impression that CINCPAC and PACAF wanted to keep the warplanes based in Thailand away from his operational influence and, by extension, that of Westmoreland and

Preparing to add further red stars to the 8th Tactical Fighter Wing MiG-kill scoreboard is Colonel Robin Olds (right), the first triple MiG-killer of the Vietnam conflict. Other victors in a May 20, 1967 encounter with MiG-17s, 40 miles (65km) north-east of Hanoi, are (left to right) Major Philip P. Combies, 1st Lt. Daniel L. Lafferty, Major John R. Pardo, 1st Lt. Stempen B. Croker and 1st Lt. Stephen A. Wayne (front center), Major Combies and Lt. Wayne having been credited with two MiGs each. Colonel Olds later went on to become the only quadruple MiG-killer of the Vietnam conflict.

55

"Rolling Thunder"

Vietnam War, 1970: CBS camera rolls as platoon comes under fire

the MACV, whom they felt to be more concerned with operations in and over South Vietnam than over North Vietnam.

Further complicating a process that was already approaching Byzantine complexity, Graham Martin and William H. Sutherland, the U.S. ambassadors to Thailand and Laos, were able to exert a certain level of political influence over operational and command arrangements. This overlapping and often ill-defined complexity, with political and supposed diplomatic factors often as important as overtly military aspects, was wholly contrary to the USAF's doctrine of having a single officer manage any air campaign, with sole responsibility within his terms of reference for the control and co-ordination of all air operations within a given theater of war. Thus it is hardly surprising that operational and tactical flexibility, and the ability to react swiftly and appropriately to a situation which could change dramatically in as little as an hour, were virtually impossible: when the 2nd Air Division in South Vietnam and Task Force 77 off the coast of Vietnam believed that a particular attack was necessary and appropriate, they were obliged to ask for authorization via PACAF and hence CINCPAC, who in turn passed the request on to the Joint Chiefs of Staff, who then solicited the comments of the Department of State and the CIA before passing the request to the White House, where decisions concerning matters of this type were made only on a weekly basis. Approval was frequently not given but even when it was, the go-ahead still had to pass back down the military chain of command to the local commanders before it could be implemented. This meant that any air

ABOVE: Aerial view, taken in 1970, of a camouflaged train, almost indistinguishable from the surrounding countryside in Communist North Vietnam, that was taken by the pilot of a USAF RF-101 Voodoo. Also visible are the rails (lower left), while the Voodoo's shadow can be seen at center right.

OPPOSITE: An antiaircraft position on a dyke, located 8 miles (13km) east of Hanoi, firing on reconnaissance aircraft.

operation schemed as a response to events on the ground or within North Vietnam was often well over a week old before approval was granted or refused, and might then be irrelevant to the situation on the ground.

The main weight of Rolling Thunder, in terms of tonnages dropped if not in sorties flown, rested on the USAF, and it quickly became clear that this branch of the U.S. armed forces was not well-prepared for the tasks demanded of it. This resulted not so much from any actions, or even inactions, by the USAF itself, but from the overriding importance which, since the late 1940s, had been placed on the U.S. forces to plan and prepare for a "third world war," with the use of nuclear weapons a likelihood rather than a possibility to protect the West against the threat of Soviet aggression. The USAF was therefore optimized for largely strategic nuclear warfare in a high-intensity, high-technology environment within countries similar to the USA in climatic conditions, and was now faced with demands to undertake a comparatively low-intensity and wholly conventional air campaign in a decidedly low-technology environment with tactical and occasionally operational level objectives, and in a region of temperatures and humidities far greater than those for which the warplanes had been designed.

The air campaign over the two Vietnams also revealed that the USAF had for too long neglected the science and practice of conventional tactics, both of these being failings which were compounded by reliance on warplanes whose overall performance, flight and armament were only poorly suited to the task. The USAF's lack of preparedness was also highlighted by the fact that the U.S. Navy and U.S. Marine Corps were altogether better prepared, and when based on an aircraft carrier also had superior conditions for aircraft maintenance and repair.

In the Grumman A-6 Intruder, the two maritime services operated the only all-weather medium-attack warplane in the US arsenal, with a pinpoint attack accuracy as a result of its advanced suite of navigation and attack electronics, and were also in the process of introducing a magnificent new warplane in the form of the McDonnell F-4 Phantom II as successor to the Vought F-8 Crusader. Though classified as a fleet defense fighter, and optimized for the carriage of missile armament and therefore not fitted, for the first time in any U.S. fighter, with inbuilt gun armament, the Phantom II had been created from an attack fighter concept, which greatly aided the type's rapid development as a true multi-role warplane. So superior was the Phantom II to anything it had in its current inventory or under final development, that the USAF had no realistic alternative but to place large orders for it in a version only little altered from its carrierborne counterpart, except for the later incorporation of a fixed gun armament in the form of a six-barrel 20-mm (0.78 inch) cannon. Thus the Phantom II emerged as the single most important warplane fielded by the U.S. forces during the course of the Vietnam War.

Once air-to-air combat had begun to occur over North Vietnam, the USAF again found itself at something of a disadvantage in terms of air-to-air armament. In this arena, and with European operations at the heart of its thinking, the USAF had long concentrated its development effort on the AIM-4 Falcon. Designed for use at medium ranges against largely non-maneuvering targets, such as bombers, the missile had a seeker unit which could be cooled to operational status only in a time as long as six seconds to secure a lock onto the target, and carried only a comparatively small and impact-fused warhead. This was effectively useless against small, maneuvering targets such as the Mikoyan-Guryevich fighters supplied to the North Vietnamese by the Soviets, and once again the USAF had to turn to the U.S. Navy, this time for its AIM-9 Sidewinder short-range and AIM-7 Sparrow medium-range missiles.

The USAF also opposed a major adaptation to the demands of the Vietnam War, which it saw largely as a short-term and atypical interruption,

"Rolling Thunder"

Although the first aircrews to reach the theater were well-experienced, the accelerating tempo of operations and arrivals in-country combined with the lengthening nature of the war to create an ever greater number of personnel, and this compounded the difficulty already being experienced in a growing inadequacy of aircrews which were both trained and experienced. Here the USAF itself intervened to worsen the problem by demanding a universal pilot-training regime and at the same time refusing to post anyone but volunteers for a second tour of combat duty. The effect of this policy was to commit rotating personnel to different aircraft types. The U.S. Navy, on the other hand, had a policy of keeping aircrew within the same basic "community" (particular types of aircraft) for the entirety of their flying careers. This ensured continuity and the retention of skills in a particular flying niche, but had a downside in the greater losses suffered by experienced crews in the course of several tours of combat flying.

Another factor which should be, but is often not, considered is the nature of the weather and other flying conditions over South-East Asia. The recurring pattern of monsoons, with their extreme humidity and heavy rainfall, meant that flying conditions were very poor for some eight months each year, in the period from late September to early May. The conditions in themselves made flying tricky, and at the same time often concealed targets in rain or fog. U.S. warplanes generally lacked adequate all-weather and night-bombing capabilities, and this meant that most U.S. air operations had to be undertaken during the day, which facilitated the task of the North Vietnamese air-defense forces, whose personnel knew that U.S. attacks would arrive only between certain

as this would have distracted the service from its "proper" task of preparing for a U.S./Soviet war. Among other things, this suggests that the USAF's higher command echelons had no conception that the Vietnam War might last for nearly 10 years.

In the Boeing B-52 Stratofortress eight-engined strategic bomber, the USAF possessed a warplane with an all-weather flight, navigation, and bombing capability, with a truly awesome bomb-carrying capacity. Believing that its use might be seen as too great an escalation of the air war, however, the Johnson administration initially refused to "bomb truck," whose control remained vested throughout in the Strategic Air Command, against any target more than a short distance north of the DMZ. In this the administration was supported by the USAF chief of staff, General John P. McConnell, who opposed the commitment of his major strategic weapon in the increasingly intense air-defense environment which North Vietnam had by now become. The operations of the B-52 force were therefore limited during the Rolling Thunder period to Route Package One close behind the DMZ.

As if this were not enough in itself, the Department of Defense created another problem by instituting a one-year rotation policy for the personnel posted to South-East Asia.

The Escalation of American Involvement in the Vietnam War

OPPOSITE: Flying an A-7 Corsair from the aircraft carrier *USS Midway (CVA41)*, Lt. J.G. Robert Noll destroyed the south span of the Phu Ly railroad bridge and caused heavy damage to another of its spans when he dropped six bombs on this rail link with Hanoi, located some 31 miles (50km) south-south-east of that city on October 7, 1966. According to his flight leader, "Bob put all six bombs right on the bridge. When the black smoke cleared the span wasn't there."

ABOVE: On August 11, 1966, bombs dropped by aircraft flying from the decks of the carrier *USS Constellation (CVA-64)* almost leveled the newly-built thermal power plant at Uong Bi.

daylight hours, and therefore had the rest of the day for maintenance, training, and rest.

The North Vietnamese know that something of this nature was inevitable, even before the launch of Rolling Thunder, and in February 1965 directed both the armed forces and the civil population to "maintain communication and transportation and to expect the complete destruction of the entire country, including Hanoi and Haiphong," and also declared a "people's war against the air war of destruction...each citizen is a soldier, each village, street, and factory a fortress on the anti-American battlefront." Hanoi was evacuated of all but the wholly

essential, with the result that by 1967 the capital's population had been halved, with those deemed not necessary to the continued functioning of Hanoi now living in rural areas.

For obvious reasons it was impossible for the North Vietnamese even to consider the possibility of winning air superiority over the U.S. air forces, and the Communist administration therefore embarked on a program of creating an air-defense system which would deny key regions of the country to U.S. attack except at the price of very high, and therefore politically unacceptable, losses to men and machines. At the beginning of Rolling Thunder, the North Vietnamese were able to deploy some

"Rolling Thunder"

1,500 antiaircraft weapons, most of which were lighter and of Soviet origin, with calibers of 37 or 57mm. Within 12 months the U.S. estimate of the number of AA guns had exceeded 5,000, including 85- and 100-mm (3.34- and 3.94 inch) radar-directed weapons. The estimate was later raised to 7,000 early in 1967 before being trimmed to fewer than 1,000 by 1972; during the Rolling Thunder campaign, however, it is reckoned that four out of five U.S. aircraft losses were attributable to antiaircraft fire.

Although the main strength of the North Vietnamese air-defense capability was vested in its antiaircraft artillery, there was also a small fighter arm which began with a mere 53 MiG-15 Fagot and MiG-17 Fresco single-engined interceptors. The U.S. air forces considered these elderly types to be obsolete and obsolescent respectively, especially as they possessed only subsonic performance. What the personnel of the U.S. air forces had not considered, however, was the way in which the North Vietnamese might be able to extract a real air-combat capability out of their aircraft. The two Soviet-supplied fighters were fast enough to undertake hit-and-run ambush operations, using the ground-controlled interception technique appropriate to the Soviet aircraft and supporting ground radars, and they also proved themselves to be more maneuverable than the American fighters, especially if they could lure the U.S. warplanes into a turning engagement, when the larger and more highly-loaded American aircraft quickly lost energy, its speed decaying to below Mach 1: in these circumstances the more lightly-loaded Soviet-supplied fighters had a decided edge in agility as well as a potent cannon armament.

Thus the U.S. air forces were amazed and dismayed when North Vietnamese fighters succeeded in shooting down notionally more capable U.S. aircraft, such as the F-8 Crusader, F-100 Super Sabre, and F-105 Thunderchief. The Americans quickly had to develop and implement new tactics to counter the greater agility of their opponents' fighters, but a more effective solution was provided by the rapid introduction of the missile-armed F-4 Phantom, which quickly became the most important fighter available to the U.S. air forces. The appearance of MiG fighters had the additional advantage for the North Vietnamese of causing U.S. airmen effectively to abort their missions as they jettisoned their bomb loads in order that they could counter the North Vietnamese fighters more effectively in the air combat arena.

In 1966, moreover, the capability of the North Vietnamese air force was considerably boosted as its initial MiG-15 and MiG-17 subsonic fighters, already supplemented by a few MiG-19 Farmer marginally **supersonic** twin-engined fighters, were

LEFT: Surrounded by undamaged farmlands and homes, the ruins of a Communist North Vietnamese supply depot smoulder after it was destroyed on April 30, 1965 by aircraft flying from the carrier USS *Midway*. Forty tons of conventional ordnance were dropped with pinpoint accuracy on the depot, which contained military supplies used against the South Vietnamese. Seventy U.S. Navy jet- and propeller-driven aircraft, striking at low altitudes, encountered only light ground fire over the target, which was photographed by a photo-reconnaissance aircraft once the clouds of black smoke had dissipated.

OPPOSITE: A collapsed bridge near Duong Phuong Thuong, bombed by aircraft from the attack aircraft carrier USS *Hancock* (CVA-19).

further reinforced with more modern Soviet-built fighters in the form of the MiG-21 Fishbed, which possessed Mach 2 performance as well as considerable agility in the air, and could thus fight on a more equal footing with the U.S. aircraft. By 1967, the North Vietnamese air force had a fighter arm averaging about 100 aircraft, many of which were based at airfields on the Chinese side of the Vietnamese-Chinese frontier, thereby facing no threat from American air attack while they were being maintained and their pilots resting.

Despite the successes of their air-defense arm, both artillery and fighters, the North Vietnamese rightly appreciated that their industrial capability and other key elements of their national economy were nonetheless vulnerable to U.S. air attack, and therefore embarked on a program of industrial and economic decentralization. As part of this effort, the larger factories, most of which were located in the delta of the Red river, were disassembled and their elements transported to naturally protected or inconspicuous locations, such as caves and apparently innocent rural villages all over the northern part of North Vietnam.

In the southern part of the country, just to the north of the DMZ, and where the main effort of the U.S. bombing campaign was concentrated, huge tunnel complexes were built deep underground, into which the populations of a great number of villages disappeared for the rest of the war. These and other measures helped the North Vietnamese to survive the worst effects of the U.S. bombing and to maintain their war effort, but what cannot be denied is that there was an acute shortage of food, especially in urban areas, as the North Vietnamese transport network lost a major part of its capacity, what was left being dominated by movement in support of the military effort. The problem was made worse by the fact that rice farmers were among those who volunteered or were drafted into military service, or as part of the growing organization required to repair the damage caused by U.S. bombing. There was also a major effort to diversify the North Vietnamese transport system, and when bridges were damaged they were quickly repaired, or when destroyed replaced by the large-scale diversion of traffic onto unpaved roads, making river crossings by means of fords, ferries, and a combination of underwater and pontoon bridges. This was a monumental effort but, as events later proved, it was all worthwhile, being durable and easily repaired, and which bombing was mostly ineffective in closing down.

The key component in this effort was the North Vietnamese population, working with enormous dedication under the most adverse of conditions. It is believed that in 1965 some 97,000 North Vietnamese volunteered for a full-time commitment to repair the damage caused by the bombing, and that between 370,000 and 500,000 more volunteered for a part-time commitment to the same task. When the North Vietnamese transport network was attacked, a number of emergency measures had been prepared for implementation in this eventuality: supplies and other matériel being moved by rail were divided into smaller loads, which were transported by rail and road convoys of small size only at night and which to air reconnaissance were of apparently little military significance. This primary logistic effort was bolstered by the delivery of other supplies and equipment by sampan, cart, wheelbarrow, and even human porterage.

When the North Vietnamese air-defense system started to introduce SAMs to supplement its already formidable array of antiaircraft artillery, U.S. pilots were faced with a difficult tactical problem: if they remained at lower altitudes they were relatively immune to the SAMs but vulnerable to the AA artillery, while opting for higher altitudes meant that they faced the reverse of the low-altitude situation, becoming easier prey to the SAMs. There was no perfect answer to this tactical conundrum, but the growing U.S. employment of electronic and other countermeasures did in fact seriously degrade the capabilities of the North Vietnamese air-defense system over time: here, one of the primary weaknesses which the U.S. forces found in the North Vietnam system was its reliance on centralized control on the basis of radar and observer information. The use of electronic countermeasures interfered severely with the performance and overall capability of the ground radars, while the use of electronic and infra-red countermeasures gradually provided a steady reduction in the ability of SAMs to hit their targets. Thus the success rate for North Vietnamese SAMs, which was in fact never very high, declined steadily from a typical figure of one kill for every 30 missiles launched in the early stages of the campaign, to one success for every 50 missiles launched later on. Even though each missile had only a low probability of success, the U.S. bombing effort paid particular attention to the missile sites and all ground elements associated with them, but the North Vietnamese never ran short of missiles.

The U.S. bombing effort had been designed to persuade the North Vietnamese government of the determination of the USA to prevent the fall of South Vietnam into the hands of the Communists, and the gradual nature of its development was intended to show that the Americans could, and indeed would, increase the weight of their effort until they achieved the result they wanted. In this it failed, and at the same time provided North Vietnam with the opportunity and the time, in the early, and less fraught stages of the campaign, to come to grips with the situation.

It is believed that by 1967 North Vietnam had 25 SAM battalions, each with six missile-launchers, and that these battalions were kept on the move between about 150 sites to make it more difficult to target them. The

The Escalation of American Involvement in the Vietnam War

time for fighter, SAM, and AA artillery units to be warned and prepared for the responses which had been decided. The North Vietnamese system may have been monolithic and cumbersome, but it did prove effective: in 1967, for example, the USA lost 248 aircraft (145 USAF, 102 U.S. Navy, and one U.S. Marine Corps) over North Vietnam.

While the numbers of U.S. aircraft committed to attacks on North Vietnam rose, so too did U.S. losses. This demanded that the USA create and implement new and more effective tactics as a matter of urgency. Large-scale attacks, which were known to the USAF as "force packages" and to the U.S. Navy as "alpha strikes," were centered on the warplanes tasked with

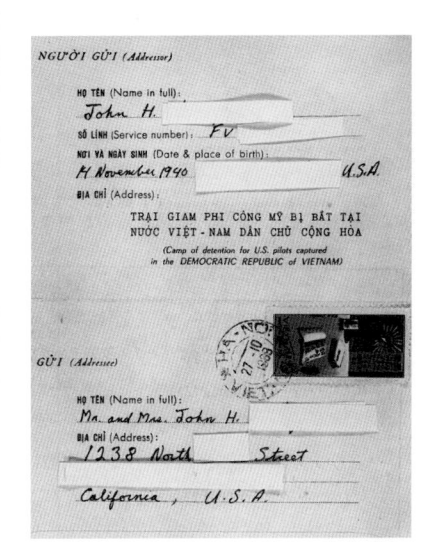

USSR also supplied the equipment and technical knowledge to allow the rapid creation of the associated radar network, which was an integrated and centralized system with more than 200 sites. This provided radar coverage of the whole of North Vietnam as well as the northern part of South Vietnam and the eastern parts of Laos and north-eastern Cambodia, allowing the central command system to track raids as they approached and entered North Vietnamese air space, providing ample

OPPOSITE: This firing of a SAM surface-to-air missile on July 5, 1966 was captured of film by a USAF RF-101 reconnaissance pilot, when North Vietnamese gunners were launching 26–28 SAMs at USAF strike pilots in an area 50–115 miles north-west of Hanoi.

ABOVE: A card sent to the parents of an American airman shot down over North Vietnam and subsequently held there in a prisoner of war camp.

RIGHT: MiG fighters on the ground on a makeshift runway.

"Rolling Thunder"

the relevant offensive action, but came to include a swelling number of support aircraft to protect the fighter-bombers and thereby allow them to complete their missions.

To pave the way for other aircraft, the target area was first entered by aircraft optimized for the "Iron Hand" defense-suppression role. These were F-105 hunter/killer teams of the "Wild Weasel" type, carrying advanced electronic systems to detect and fix the location of the radars associated with SAM guidance and control, and also electronic countermeasures for self-protection. The aircraft controlled attacks to suppress AA artillery and carried AGM-45 Shrike anti-radiation missiles, another weapon type created for the U.S. Navy to home in on SAM radar systems. The SA-2 SAM possessed greater range than the Shrike, but if the Shrike was launched and the radar remained active to guide the missile, the Shrike homed in on the signal and destroyed its source. The development of the Iron Hand concept then led to the emergence of a see-saw development race of increasing technical sophistication between the North Vietnamese radar operators and the crews of the Wild Weasel aircraft. While the Iron Hand role was particular to the USAF, the U.S. Navy proceeded along an analogous path without the creation of specialized units.

ABOVE: The nuclear-powered attack aircraft carrier USS Enterprise (CVAN-65) comes alongside the fast-combat support ship USS Sacramento (AOE-1) in the Gulf of Tonkin for underway replenishment. The Sacramento functioned as an oiler, ammunition, and refrigerated stores ship, all rolled into one.

OPPOSITE: Lt. J.G. Charles Hartman and Lt. Cdr. Edwin Greathouse show RADM William F. Bringle how they shot down a MIG-17 during a mission over North Vietnam.

The Escalation of American Involvement in the Vietnam War

With the North Vietnamese ground-based defense system either destroyed or forced to shut down for fear of obliteration, the target area was then deemed safe enough to be entered by the attack aircraft with their loads of different bombs, although their vulnerability in the bomb-laden stage was reflected in their support by fighters operating in the CAP (combat air patrol) or MiGCAP role, and other aircraft carrying the electronic jamming gear to ensure further degradation of the North Vietnamese radar capability. Throughout the Vietnam War, new ECM systems were being designed and built in the USA in an almost endless stream of equipments and upgrades to existing equipments, and rushed to South Vietnam and Thailand as soon as they were deemed sufficiently combat-capable. It was in matters such as this that the U.S. was able to exploit its great technological capabilities and industrial ability to get systems into production very rapidly: the problem was that large numbers of these equipments were technologically successful in boosting the protection of attack packages, but technically incapable of surviving the humidity and poor servicing facilities of South-East Asia for all but the shortest of times.

Other elements of the U.S. concept of missions penetrating North Vietnamese air space were Boeing KC-135 Stratotanker inflight-refueling facilities, a steadily improving progression of combat search and rescue helicopters (with increasing amounts of armor and guns) to find and rescue downed airmen, and aircraft to protect the SAR helicopters. This last fixed-wing type was usually the A-1 Skyraider, piston-engined and with performance that did not exceed that of its charges by any great degree, being of long endurance and with the capability of carrying the large and diverse weapons to tackle Communist forces trying to reach downed men before the arrival of the helicopter, and then suppressing any fire which the opposition might loft in an attempt to

65

"Rolling Thunder"

down the SAR helicopter and capture or kill the downed men. This combat SAR capability was of great significance to the U.S. forces, not only for recovering downed men but also in raising the morale of airmen, who could be confident that they would no longer be left to the mercies of the Communist ground forces.

Despite the fact that Rolling Thunder was manifestly failing to achieve the result it had been created to produce, between mid-1966 and the final stages of 1967 Johnson and McNamara continued to authorize attacks on new and important targets only on a one by one basis, at the same time using this tactic as evidence to opponents of the war in the U.S. Congress, and indeed inside the administration, that they had only limited objectives which they were tackling with strictly limited resources. This palliative effort also included the occasional scaling-back of the bombing, together with a number of low-key attempts to lure the North Vietnamese into peace talks.

Despite the USA's introduction of technical aids, better weapons, and tactics, and the combat SAR force, the very fact that it had to overfly North Vietnam to attack targets, which then had to be attacked again on a frequent basis, began to have an adverse effect on the morale of aircrews. After a fact-finding visit to South Vietnam during September 1966, Admiral David McDonald, the Chief of Naval Operations, informed the other members of the Joint Chiefs of Staff committee that the men involved in Rolling Thunder were angered by the nature of the target-selection process, and felt that the entire operation had been wrongly conceived in establishing "guidelines requiring repetitive air programs that seemed more than anything else to benefit enemy gunners." In 1967, which was the

ABOVE: Gulf of Tonkin. A catapult crewman aboard the attack aircraft carrier USS *America* (CVA-66) watches as two bomb-laden A-7A Corsair II attack aircraft head out to sea following their launch from the flight deck.

OPPOSITE: Guided under radar control by a B-66 Destroyer, USAF F-4C Phantom crews return to drop bombs on Communist military targets after the longest lull in the Vietnam air war.

second complete year of Rolling Thunder, the USA lost 362 aircraft (208 USAF, 142 U.S. Navy, and 12 U.S. Marine Corps) over North Vietnam.

The years 1967 and 1968 saw Rolling Thunder attain its final form, in which the object of the entire operation, especially in the higher-numbered route packages on North Vietnam's northern regions, became the interdiction of the quantities of supplies and matériel flowing into North Vietnam for local purposes as well as for further dissemination to the Communist forces operating in South Vietnam, and the comprehensive destruction of North Vietnam's industrial and economic infrastructure relevant to the military effort. In this period the majority of U.S. warplane losses resulted from AA artillery fire, but SAMs and North Vietnamese fighters also became an increasing threat to workhorses of the bombing effort, such as the USAF's F-105 Thunderchief and U.S. Navy's Douglas A-4 Skyhawk. The MiG-19 and MiG-21 became an increasing problem, not only because of the greater combat experience now possessed by their North Vietnamese pilots but also because U.S. radar coverage of North Vietnam did not include the Red river delta, a primary target area for the Americans and one in which the North Vietnamese could get their fighters into the air in good time to "bounce" unsuspecting U.S. warplanes. The problem was compounded by the fact that the radar of U.S. airborne early-warning aircraft was not picking out these small fighters at low altitude in the clutter of ground returns, and the North Vietnamese fighters were also hard to spot visually because of their small size.

It was not all one-way traffic in air combat, however, and it should be noted that F-105 pilots achieved 27 air combat "kills," giving North Vietnamese and U.S. successes nearly equal parity. In January 1967 the Americans did manage to catch the MiG fighters completely off balance and score a useful success in the course of Operation Bolo. In this, F-4 Phantom multi-role fighters used the same radio call signs, as well as the approach vector, altitude, and speed, as a typical flight of fully loaded F-105 fighter-bombers, so luring the North Vietnamese fighters into an attack on what was an altogether more formidable group of warplanes: during a 12-minute engagement, the

"Rolling Thunder"

Phantoms shot down seven MiG fighters without loss to themselves.

The U.S. air forces began what was as yet their most intensive and sustained effort late in 1967, in the hope of forcing North Vietnam into peace negotiations. By this stage of Rolling Thunder, almost every target authorized to the Joint Chiefs of Staff had come under air attack, the targets including airfields which had earlier been on the prohibited list. Only central Hanoi, Haiphong, and the North Vietnamese-Chinese border were declared inviolable in this latest stage of the offensive, in which the core of the U.S. plan was the isolation of North Vietnam's cities and major towns by the destruction of bridges and the severing of communications networks. Other targets included the Thai Nguyen steel manufacturing complex, electricity-generating facilities, ship and railway repair workshops, and warehouse complexes. The gravity of the offensive was such that the North Vietnamese fighters were committed in large numbers to the defense of Hanoi, the kill ratio falling to one U.S. warplane for every two MiG fighters.

During 1968, the North Vietnamese fighters were responsible for shooting down 22 percent of the 139 U.S. warplanes (75 USAF, 59 U.S. Navy, and five U.S. Marine Corps) lost over the north. This was the main reason why U.S. attacks were finally authorized on the last North Vietnamese airfields, whose bombing had previously been banned. Despite the commitment which the USA poured into Rolling Thunder, and the devastation caused in North Vietnam, the Communist forces in South Vietnam were still very potent, as indicated on January 30, 1968, when they started their largest land offensive yet, lashing out at targets throughout South Vietnam during the lunar New Year holiday. This Tet Offensive saw some of the war's most bitter fighting, but ended as a major operational and tactical defeat for the North Vietnamese and their South Vietnamese Communist allies; at the same time it was a major strategic and psychological victory for the Communists as the American people, long assured that the war would soon end in a major victory for the U.S. and South Vietnamese forces, now saw that the task was in fact still very much in the balance, with much time and many casualties to be endured in the future if victory was indeed to be won. The antiwar movement in the USA grew ever more strident and began to spread ever wider, and indeed psychologically deeper, into the U.S. population at large. This had obvious ramifications for the politicians in Washington, where the determination of the administration and legislature alike was severely weakened.

Fortunately for North Vietnam, many of the believers in the U.S. bombing policy were convinced it would be unwise to risk its primary strategic bomber, the B-52, over North Vietnam, even though this was the one available warplane with the capacity to deliver huge tonnages of bombs with great accuracy under all weather conditions by day and by night. Without the commitment of the B-52 there was no way in which the U.S. air forces could escalate their air effort in response to the Tet Offensive, for the seasonal bad weather made it impossible to undertake any but small-scale tactical warplane operations until the advent of better conditions in April.

By the spring of 1967, McNamara and other civilian leaders of the Johnson administration were now gloomily sure that Rolling Thunder and the ground war in South Vietnam were failing. The bombing campaign had clearly failed either to force North Vietnam to its knees militarily or economically, or persuade the Communist administration to come to the negotiating table. There was a distinct feeling of war-weariness in Washington, and many of those who felt that way were in a position to oppose the recommendations of the Joint Chiefs of Staff, both to increase the pace and weight of the air war against North Vietnam and to loosen the restrictions imposed on the military with regard to target selection. In this respect the military leadership now found itself in an impossible situation of its own making: the generals and admirals had long stated they were winning the war over North Vietnam, but were now asking for a relaxation of the targeting policy precisely so that the air campaign would in fact now succeed. To any but the willfully blind, it was now altogether clear that there was a total incompatibility between the restriction to limited goals resulting from U.S. foreign policy and the objective of total victory now espoused by the military leadership. What no one could answer, of course, was the thorny problem of now to defeat the Communist forces in South Vietnam, sponsored by North Vietnam, without wholly defeating North Vietnam itself.

On August 9, 1967 the Armed Services Committee of the U.S. Senate opened hearings on the bombing campaign, largely as a result of the complaints received by a number of senators from members of the armed

OPPOSITE: Aircraft of the attack carrier Air *Wing Nine* (CVW-9) in the Gulf of Tonkin wait on the after flight deck of the attack aircraft carrier USS Constellation (CV-64) to be launched on air strikes in the Haiphong area of North Vietnam.

"Rolling Thunder"

HANOI/BAC MAI AIRFIELD

4 DESTROYED SUPPORT BUILDINGS
6 DESTROYED SUPPORT BUILDINGS
RUNWAY INTERDICTED
10 DESTROYED BARRACKS

ABOVE: Military target area 12 in Operation Linebacker was the Hanoi/Bac Mai airfield.

forces. The members of the Joint Chiefs of Staff testified before the committee, making critical comments about the graduated nature of the air war and the restrictions imposed on the conduct of purely military matters by civilians reacting to political and diplomatic events. What they wanted, the military advised, was to be set a task by the administration, and then to be freed to secure the attainment of the stated objective by the best means available to them. It was clear that McNamara, as the only civilian subpoenaed and the last to be asked to testify, was to be the scapegoat. McNamara was too astute a wheeler and dealer to be caught in this fashion, however, and neatly stated his objections to an unlimited air war while also rebutting the claims of the military. There was an almost prophetic ring to McNamara's admission that there was "no basis to believe that any bombing campaign...would by itself force Ho Chi Minh's regime into submission, short, that is, of the virtual annihilation of North Vietnam and its people." It was now obvious to Johnson, though, that McNamara was now a major liability to his administration, and in February 1968 McNamara resigned and was replaced by Clark Clifford, a personal friend of Johnson and a long-standing opponent of McNamara's recommendations that U.S. troop numbers in South Vietnam be stabilized and Rolling Thunder terminated.

Adding to the administration's problems, however, was the fact that McNamara's position was almost immediately adopted by Dean Rusk, the Secretary of State, and up to now a strong believer in Rolling Thunder. Rusk proposed limiting the campaign to the panhandle of North Vietnam just above the DMZ, without preconditions, and awaiting North Vietnam's response. But within just a few months, Clifford also changed tack and adopted McNamara's position, in the process slowly but steadily becoming a proponent of the concept that the USA had to withdraw from its open-ended commitment to South Vietnam.

Disappointed by political defeats at home and hoping that North Vietnam would enter into negotiations, on March 31, 1968 Johnson announced the end of all bombing north of the 19th parallel. Thus the U.S. air forces now concentrated all the offensive effort which had previously been spread over the whole of North Vietnam into the smaller region between the 17th and 19th parallels. The USAF increased the number of sorties sent into Route Package One by 100 percent, which entailed more than 6,000 sorties now being flown against movement "chokepoints," the destruction of roads, and the hunting and destroying of truck traffic. The North Vietnamese response was a doubling of the number of AA artillery batteries in the panhandle region of North Vietnam, though most of the SAM battalions were left in position around Hanoi and Haiphong.

Despite its earlier ultimatum that it would not enter negotiations while the bombing continued, North Vietnam finally agreed to a meeting with a U.S. delegation in Paris for preliminary talks. Johnson then announced that there would be a complete halt to the Rolling Thunder bombing of North Vietnam from November 1, 1968, a date just before the U.S. presidential election. This bombing halt was linked with the achievement of progress in the peace talks, but the Joint Chiefs of Staff believed that the administration would not order a resumption of the bombing campaign under any circumstances and, as events were to prove, they were right.

In the period of Rolling Thunder between March 1965 and November 1968, USAF warplanes flew 153,784 sorties against North Vietnam, and the U.S. Navy and U.S. Marine Corps added 152,399 more. On December 31, 1967, the Department of Defense announced that, at 864,000 tons, the weight of bombs dropped on North Vietnam during Rolling Thunder was greater than that dropped in the entire Korean War, and greater still than in the Pacific campaign of the Second World War. On January 1, 1968 the CIA revealed an estimate suggesting that U.S.$370 million of damage had been inflicted on North Vietnam in terms of the physical destruction caused by the bombing, this figure including US$164 million of damage to fixed assets, such as factories, bridges, and electricity-generating stations. The report also estimated North Vietnamese casualties of 1,000 per week, which added up to some 90,000, including 72,000 civilians, for the 44-month duration of the campaign.

Combat and operational losses suffered by the U.S. air forces totaled 526 USAF, 397 U.S. Navy, and 19 U.S. Marine Corps aircraft over or near North Vietnam. Some 745 men had been downed with these aircraft, and of these USAF recorded 145 rescued, 255 killed, 222 captured (of whom 23 died in captivity), and 123 missing. Equivalent U.S. Navy and U.S. Marine Corps figures are more problematical, but during the 44 months of the operation 454 naval aviators were killed, captured, or posted missing during operations over North Vietnam and Laos.

Rolling Thunder had been an undertaking designed to exert psychological and physical pressure, but had rapidly become a tactical and operational campaign of interdiction. It failed for two main reasons, both of them linked directly to the civilian and military policy-makers in the USA: firstly, neither ever conceived that North Vietnam would or indeed could survive under the weight of bombs which was to be dropped on it, and the civilian element also lacked the understanding of air power to comprehend that its policies were nugatory in terms of effective use of air power; secondly, the U.S. military leadership signally failed, right from the start, to propose, develop, and later press for the adoption of strategy apposite to the situation in Vietnam.

It should also be recorded that Rolling Thunder suffered from the same deadening "managerial" attitude to decision-making as did the rest of the U.S. military effort in South-East Asia. Thus it was the number of sorties generated which became the measure by which the campaign was judged, regardless of the fact that the number of sorties made and the tonnages of bombs dropped might have been useful in judging levels of efficiency, but were certainly not useful in estimating progress toward a stated aim. Throughout this time, North Vietnam remained a formidable enemy as a result of its own strengths and determination, aided by the physical and diplomatic support of China and the USSR.

Text-Dependent Questions

1. What was Operation Rolling Thunder?

2. How long did Operation Rolling Thunder last?

3. Was Operation Rolling Thunder a success or failure?

Research Projects

Explain how the North Vietnamese reduced the impact of American bombing raids during the Vietnam War.

TIME LINE OF THE VIETNAM WAR

1858 French colonial rule begins.

1930 Ho Chi Minh founds the Indochinese Communist Party (ICP).

1941 ICP organises a guerrilla force, Viet Minh, in response to invasion by Japan during World War II.

1945 The Viet Minh seizes power. Ho Chi Minh announces Vietnam's independence.

1946 French forces attack Viet Minh in Haiphong in November, sparking the war of resistance against the colonial power.

1950 Democratic Republic of Vietnam is recognised by China and USSR.

1954 Viet Minh forces attack an isolated French military outpost in the town of Dien Bien Phu. The attempt to take the outpost lasts two months, during which time the French government agrees to peace talks in Geneva.

Vietnam is split into North and South at Geneva conference.

1956 South Vietnamese President Ngo Dinh Diem begins campaign against political dissidents.

1957 Beginning of Communist insurgency in the South.

1959 Weapons and men from North Vietnam begin infiltrating the South.

1960 American aid to Diem increased.

1962 Number of U.S. military advisors in South Vietnam rises to 12,000.

1963 Viet Cong, the communist guerrillas operating in South Vietnam, defeat units of the ARVN, the South Vietnamese Army.

President Diem is overthrown and then killed in a U.S.-backed military coup.

U.S. ENTERS THE WAR

1964 Gulf of Tonkin incident: the U.S. says North Vietnamese patrol boats fire on two U.S. Navy destroyers. U.S. Congress approves Gulf of Tonkin Resolution, authorising military action in region.

1965 200,000 American combat troops arrive in South Vietnam.

1966 U.S. troop numbers in Vietnam rise to 400,000, then to 500,000 the following year.

1968 Tet Offensive - a combined assault by Viet Cong and the North Vietnamese army on U.S. positions - begins. More than 500 civilians die in the U.S. massacre at My Lai. Thousands are killed by communist forces during their occupation of the city of Hue.

1969 Ho Chi Minh dies. President Nixon begins to reduce U.S. ground troops in Vietnam as domestic public opposition to the war grows.

1970 Nixon's national security advisor, Henry Kissinger, and Le Duc Tho, for the Hanoi government, start talks in Paris.

1973 Ceasefire agreement in Paris, U.S. troop pull-out completed by March.

1975 North Vietnamese troops invade South Vietnam and take control of the whole country after South Vietnamese President Duong Van Minh surrenders.

OPPOSITE: The U.S. Navy aircraft carrier USS *Midway* (CVA-41) underway. Midway, with assigned Carrier Air Wing 2, was deployed to Vietnam from March 6–November 23, 1965.

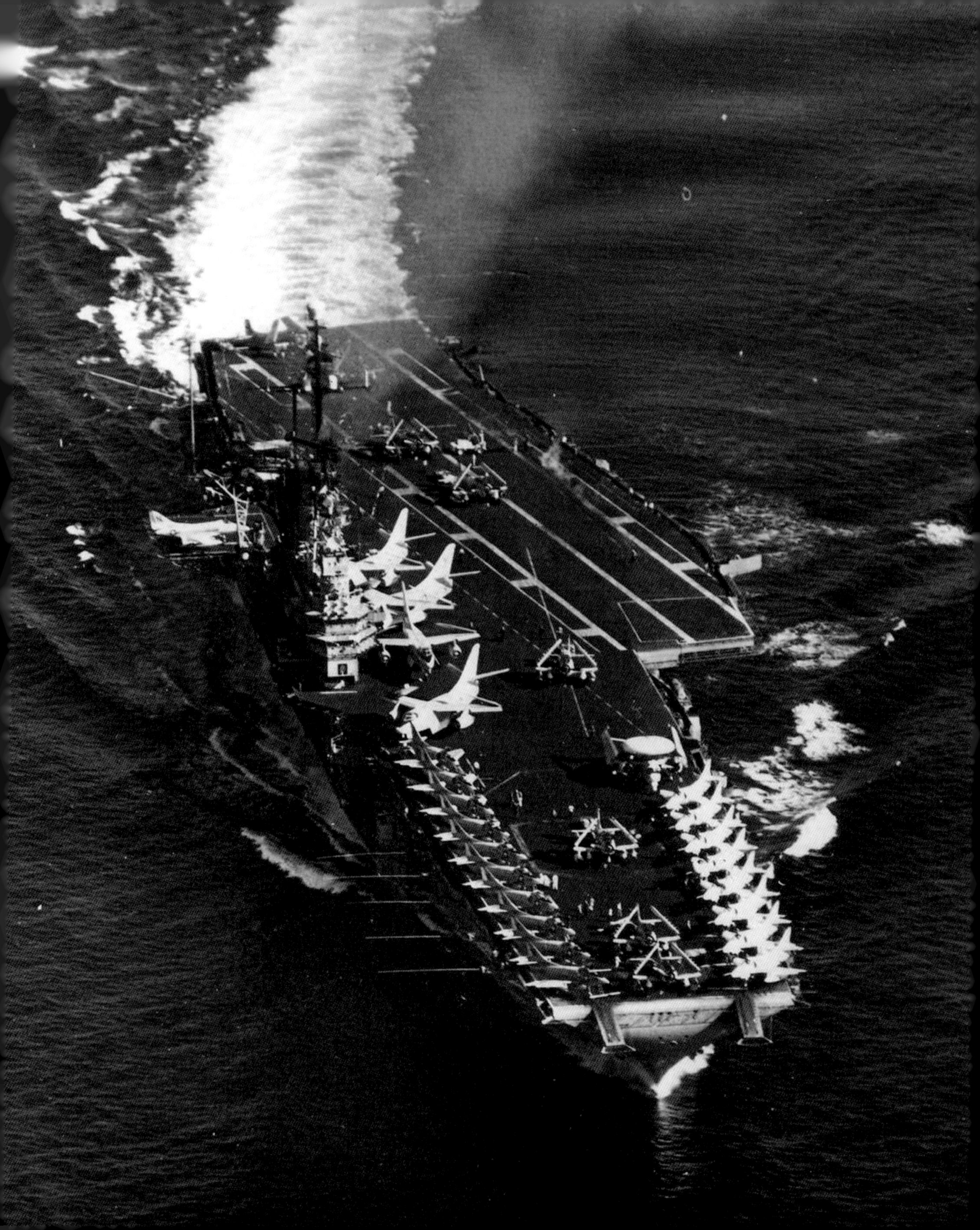

Series Glossary of Key Terms

ARVN Army of the Republic of Vietnam.

Boat People A term given to refugees fleeing Vietnam following the Communist takeover.

Body Count The number of enemy soldiers killed in an engagement.

Charlie, Charles or **Mr Charlie** Slang for the Viet Cong.

Chopper Helicopter.

Containment U.S. government policy to prevent the spread of Communism.

Demilitarized Zone (DMZ) The line that divided North Vietnam and South Vietnam, located at the 17th parallell.

Domino Theory A chain of events describing a situation when one country falls to Communism, others will follow.

DRV Acronym for Democratic Republic of Vietnam.

Friendly Fire An accidental attack on one's own military forces.

Gulf of Tonkin Incident Two attacks by North Vietnam against U.S. destroyers *USS Maddox* and *USS Turner Joy*.

Ho Chi Minh Trail Supply paths used by Communist forces to supply troops fighting in the South.

Irregulars Armed individuals or groups not members of regular armed forces.

Napalm A defoliant chemical dispersed by bombs or flamethrowers, used to destroy foliage in order to expose enemy troops.

Post-traumatic Stress Disorder A psychological disorder caused by experiencing trauma. Symptoms include flashbacks, nightmares, lack of sleep, and other psychological problems.

POW Acronym for prisoner of war.

MIA Acronym for missing in action.

Tet Offensive A large scale attack on South Vietnam by North Vietnam's army and the Viet Cong.

Tonkin Northern section of Vietnam.

Tunnel Rats Soldiers who explored the network of tunnels constructed by the Viet Cong.

Viet Cong Communist guerrilla forces in South Vietnam.

Viet Minh League for the Independence of Vietnam established by Ho Chi Minh.

Vietnamization The process of withdrawing U.S. troops from Vietnam and turning over combat to the South Vietnamese.

Further Reading and Internet Resources

WEBSITES

http://spartacus-educational.com/VietnamWar.htm

http://www.history.com/topics/vietnam-war

https://www.britannica.com/event/Vietnam-War

http://www.historynet.com/vietnam-war

BOOKS

Hourly History. *Vietnam War: A History From Beginning to End,* Hourly History Ltd., 2016. Kindle edition 2016.

Mark Atwood Lawrence. *The Vietnam War: A Concise International History.* Oxford University Press, 2010

Stuart Murray. *DK Eyewitness Books: Vietnam War. DK Publishing Inc.*, 2005.

If you enjoyed this book take a look at Mason Crest's other war series:

The Civil War, World War II, Major U.S. Historical Wars.

Index

Page numbers in ***bold italics*** refer to photographs and their captions or to videos.

A

A-1 Skyraider, *12–13*, *54*, 65
A-4 Skyhawk, *40–41*, *42–43*, 67
A-6 Intruder, 57
A-7 Corsair, *58–59*
A-7 Corsair II, *66*
advisers, definition of, 12
aerial encounters, 52–53
AGM-45 Shrike missiles, 64
AIM-4 Falcon, 57
AIM-7 Sparrow, 57
AIM-9 Sidewinder, 57
Air Component Command, 55
Air Wing Nine, *67*
air-defense system, 59–60
air-to-air combat, 57, 60–61, 67, 69
ally, definition of, 12
alpha strikes, 63–64
anitwar movement in US, 69
AOE-1, *64*
armed reconnaissance, 51
Armed Services Committee hearings, 69–70

B

B-52 Stratofortress, 58
B-57 bombers, 43
B-66 Destroyer, *52*, *66–67*
Baria-Long Khanh, 33
Bell UH-1 Huey, *22*
Binh Duong province, *38*
Binh Gia, Battle of, 32–33, 35, 37–38
Binh Long-Phuoc Long, 33
Bringle, William F., *64–65*
Brink Hotel, 29
Buddhists, 12, 31
Bundy, McGeorge, 41
Bundy, William P., 39

C

Camp Bunard, *20*
Camp Holloway, 40–41
Camp Trai Trung Sup, *16*
Cape Vinh Son, 15
casualties, 29, 35, 38, 71
China, support from, 47
CINCPAC, 55–56
Civilian Irregular Defense Group (CIDG), *16*, *30–31*, 38
Clifford, Clark, 70
Combat Sky Spot mission, *52*
Combies, Philip P., 55
command structures, 55–57
coup attempt, 43
Croker, Stempen B., 55
CV-64, *67*
CVA-19, *60–61*
CVA-41, *58–59*
CVA-64, *44–45*, *59*
CVA-66, *66*
CVAN-65, *42–43*, *64*
CVW-9, *67*

D

Da Nang, 53
Daniel, Robert, *30–31*
Dat Do, 35
defense-suppression techniques, 64–65
Democratic Republic of Vietnam (DRV), 47–48
Dong Hoi, 41, 43
Dong Xoai, 38
Duong Phuong Thuong, *60–61*

F

F-4 Phantom, 60, 67, 69
F-4C Phantom, *66–67*
F-8 Crusader, *43*, *44–45*, 57, 60
F-100 Super Sabre, *50–51*, 60
F-105 Thunderchief, *50–51*, *52*, 53–54, 60, 64, 67
flying conditions, 58–59
force packages, 63–64
Forward Command Committee, 33

G

Gallant, Thomas G., *20*
Galvin, Marcelino, *34*

Geneva Accords, 15
Greathouse, Edwin, *64–65*
Gulf of Tonkin, photograph of, *64*, *66*, *67*
Gulf of Tonkin incident
  context for, 13, 15
  description of, 12, 15–16, 18, 24
  Johnson's speech regarding, *24*, *28*
  photograph of, *17*
Gulf of Tonkin Resolution, 12, 18, *25*

H

Haiphong, 49, *67*, 69
Hanoi, 59, 69
Hanoi/Bac Mai airfield, *68*
Harkin, 28
Hartman, J. G. Charles, *64–65*
Herrick, John J., *14*, 16
High National Council (HNC), 25, 28, 31
Ho Chi Minh, death of, *35*
Hoai Duc, 35
Hon Nieu, 15
Huong. *See* Tran Van Huong

I

insurgents, number of, 18, 20
International Control Commission, 15
Iron Hand concept, 64

J

Jaudon, Arnold S., *38*
Johnson, Lyndon B.
  concerns over China and USSR, 47, 49
  end of Rolling Thunder and, 71
  growth of U.S. involvement and, 13, 20–22
  Gulf of Tonkin incident and, 12, 18, *24*, *25*, *28*
  McNamara and, 70
  order to retaliate from, 41
  photograph of, *3–4*, *24*
  POL targets and, 54

76

refusal to attack and, 29, 31
Rolling Thunder and, 45
strategy and, 22–23, 39
target selection and, 50, 66

K

KC-135 Stratotanker, 65
Kennedy administration, 12–13
Khanh, 22, 25, 28–29, 31–32, 43
Korat, 49
Kosygin, Alexei, 41
Ky. *See* Nguyen Cao Ky

L

Lafferty, Daniel L., *55*
Laos, escalation of war and, 23
Le Trong Tan, 33
leaflet drops, *20*
Long Thanh, 35

M

M113 Armed Personnel Carrier, *31*, 35
March North land campaign, 22
Martin, Graham, 56
McConnell, John P., 58
McDonald, David, 66
McDonnell F-4 Phantom II, 57
McNamara, Robert S., 15, 18, 47, 48, 50, 66, 69, 70
MiG (Mikoyan-Gureyvich) fighters, *63*, 69
 MiG-15 Fagot, 60
 MiG-17, *55*, *64–65*
 MiG-17 Fresco, 60
 MiG-19 Farmer, 60, 67
 MiG-21, *48–49*, 67
 MiG-21 Fishbed, 61
Mikoyan-Gureyvich fighter, *12–13*
Mikoyan-Gureyvich MiG-15 fighters, 53, 57
Military Assistance Command, Vietnam (MACV), 15, 21, *38*, 55–56
Momyer, William, 55–56
Morrison, Stephen, 15

N

Nam Bo Regional Command, 33
National Liberation Front (NLF), 32–33, 38
news footage, *56*
Nguyen Cao Ky, 25, 28
Nguyen Chi Thanh, 33
Nhon Trach, 35
Noll, J. G. Robert, *58–59*
Nui Ba Den, *17*

O

Ogier, Commander, *14*
Olds, Robin, *55*
Operation 34A, 13, 15
Operation Barrel Roll, 23, 25, 43
Operation Bolo, 67, 69
Operation Flaming Dart I, 41, 43, 47
Operation Flaming Dart II, 41, 47
Operation Helping Hand, 32
Operation Linebacker, *68*
Operation Market Time, *4–5*
Operation Rolling Thunder, 41, 43, 45–52, *46–47*, 55–57, 59–60, 66–67, 69–71

P

PACAF, 55–56
Pardo, John R., *55*
Paris, James R., *38*
Paris talks, 71
Phan Huy Quat, 43
Phan Khac Suu, 25
Phan Rang airbase, *50–51*
Phu Ly railroad, *58–59*
Pleiku, 41, 47
POL (petroleum, oil, and lubricant) facilities, 54–55
prisoners of war, *50*, *63*
Provincial Health Assistance Program (PHAP), *28*

Q

Quang Binh province, *46*
Quang Khe, 48
Quang Trach district, *46*

Quang Tri province, *28–29*
Qui Nhon, 41, 47

R

RF-101 Voodoo, *56*, *62–63*
rotating personnel, 58
Rouly, Alvin J., *16*
route packages, 49–50
Rusk, Dean, 29, 70

S

Saigon, defense of, *36–37*
SAMs (surface-to-air missiles), 62–63, *62–63*, 64, 71
search and rescue (SAR) helicopters, 65–66
self-immolation, 32
Sharp, Ulysses Simpson Grant, Jr., *14–15*, 15
South Vietnam, U.S. targets in, 43
Southeast Asia Collective Defense Treaty, 18
South-East Asia Resolution, 12
SP-5B Marlin, *4–5*
Strategic Air Command, 58
supersonic fighters, 60–61
surface-to-air missile batteries, 53–54, 62–64, 67
Sutherland, William H., 56
Suu. *See* Phan Khac Suu

T

Takhli Royal Thai Air Force Base, 49, *52*
targets, selection of, 48, 50, 66–67
Taylor, Maxwell D., 21–23, 28–29, 38–39, 41
Tet Offensive, 69
Tet Truce, 40
Thai Hung, *34*
Thua Thien, *30–31*
Tran Sup checkpoint, *38*
Tran Van Huong, 25, 31–32
transportation system, attacks on, 47, 50, *54*, *59*, *60–61*, 61–62, 69
tunnel systems, 61

Index

U
Ubon, 49
Udon thani, 49
U.S. Medical Civic Action Program (MEDCAP), *34*
USAF, lack of preparedness of, 57–58
USS *America*, *66*
USS *Bon Homme Richard*, 15
USS *Constellation*, 18, *44–45*, *59*, *67*
USS *Enterprise*, *42–43*, *64*
USS *Hancock*, *60–61*
USS *Maddox*, 12, *12*, *14*, 15–16, *17*, 24, *24*
USS *Midway*, *58–59*, *60*
USS *Sacramento*, *64*
USS *Ticonderoga*, 16, 18
USS *Turner Joy*, 12, 16, 24
USSR, 47, 53, 63

V
Viet Cong
　advance of, 33–35
　attack by, 29, 40–41
　at Binh Gia, 32–33, 35, 37–38
Vietnam People's Air Force, *48–49*
Vietnam People's Army, *41*
Vietnam Veterans Memorial Wall, *10*, 11
Vietnamese Special Forces (LLDB), *16*
Vinh, 41

W
Wayne, Stephen A., *55*
Westmoreland, William C., 25, 28, 38–39, 45, 46, 55–56
Wheeler, Earl G., 49

X
Xom Bang, 48

Y
Yankee Station, 49
Young Turks, 25, 28–29, 31–32

OPPOSITE: An officer examines the entrance to a NLF bunker complex. The Communist forces were notably adept at constructing and using such complexes in many parts of South Vietnam.

The Escalation of American Involvement in the Vietnam War

PHOTOGRAPHIC ACKNOWLEDGEMENTS

All images in this book are supplied by Cody Images and are in the public domain.

The content of this book was first published as *VIETNAM WAR*.

ABOUT THE AUTHOR
Christopher Chant

Christopher Chant is a successful writer on aviation and modern military matters, and has a substantial number of authoritative titles to his credit. He was born in Cheshire, England in December 1945, and spent his childhood in East Africa, where his father was an officer in the Colonial Service. He returned to the UK for his education at the King's School, Canterbury (1959–64) and at Oriel College, Oxford (1964–68).

Aviation in particular and military matters in general have long been a passion, and after taking his degree he moved to London as an assistant editor on the Purnell partworks, *History of the Second World War* (1968–69) and *History of the First World War* (1969–72). On completion of the latter he moved to Orbis Publishing as editor of the partwork, *World War II* (1972–74), on completion of which he decided to become a freelance writer and editor.

Living first in London, then in Lincolnshire after his marriage in 1978, and currently in Sutherland, at the north-western tip of Scotland, he has also contributed as editor and writer to the partworks, *The Illustrated Encyclopedia of Aircraft*, *War Machine*, *Warplane*, *Take-Off*, *World Aircraft Information Files* and *World Weapons*, and to the magazine *World Air Power Journal*. In more recent years he was also involved in the creation of a five-disk CR-ROM series, covering the majority of the world's military aircraft from World War I to the present, and also in the writing of scripts for a number of video cassette and TV programs, latterly for Continuo Creative.

As sole author, Chris has more than 90 books to his credit, many of them produced in multiple editions and co-editions, including more than 50 on aviation subjects. As co-author he has contributed to 15 books, ten of which are also connected with aviation. He has written the historical narrative and technical database for a five-disk *History of Warplanes* CD-ROM series, and has been responsible for numerous video cassette programs on military and aviation matters, writing scripts for several TV programmes and an A–Z 'All the World's Aircraft' section in Aerospace/Bright Star *World Aircraft Information Files* partwork. He has been contributing editor to a number of books on naval, military and aviation subjects as well as to numerous partworks concerned with military history and technology. He has also produced several continuity card sets on aircraft for publishers such as Agostini, Del Prado, Eaglemoss, Edito-Service and Osprey.